The Dinosaur Among Us

JEFFREY C. HOOKE

THE DINOSAUR AMONG US
The World Bank and
Its Path to Extinction

2007

The Dinosaur Among Us

TABLE OF CONTENTS

Page

ACKNOWLEDGEMENTS

I want to thank my wife, Patty, and my two sons, Matt and Greg, for their understanding during the preparation of this book. I also want to convey my appreciation to Alex Hooke and Tom Firey, who supplied interesting viewpoints. Sue Carlin has my gratitude for her help in word processing the manuscript. A special thanks to David Young for his work on the exhibits. And finally, my gratefulness to the BookSurge editorial and production team: Hugh Henry, Sarah Sutherland, Kristin Loke, and Julie Burnett.

I.
A DAY IN THE LIFE

It is a bright June morning in Washington. The sun is shining and the spring flowers are in bloom. There is a mild breeze, causing the flags adorning the embassies, monuments, and buildings to flutter gently. The capital's parks and wide boulevards beckon the stream of commuters into the downtown core.

At the corner of 18th Street and Pennsylvania Avenue sits the World Bank headquarters, an imposing edifice occupying an entire city block. Expanded in the early 1990's at a cost of $300 million, the building has ceased to house even one-third of the Bank's employees, who are spread out over eight properties in the area and dozens more worldwide. Inside the building's massive, 12 story atrium, hang the flags of its members, a moving testament to the hope that countries can work together in solving economic problems. Upstairs, the Board Room is particularly striking. Covering 5,000 square feet, it features a 27 foot high curved ceiling and a 50 foot cantilevered conference table. The effect is of a developmental Valhalla where the gods meet to deliberate on the day's great issues.

As 9:00 a.m. approaches, Bank employees flash their ID cards at the entrance doors and pass guards to reach the cavernous lobby. The ethnic and racial diversity of the group is striking, reflecting the Bank's attempt to recruit individuals from all member countries. A few of the arrivals for work that day retain their native costume, giving the procession a colorful, festive tone.

A small crowd gathers near the elevators. Conversations, while polite, are short. Most employees endure long commutes and are in no mood to talk. A popular address seems to be Fairfax County, an affluent Virginia suburb, about 10 miles from downtown. Statistically, Fairfax is the second richest county in the United States by median income, and a single-family home fetches a median price of $425,000. This housing expense is easily affordable within the Bank's mid-level salary ranges, and high-level managers often select the toney suburb of McLean, known for its spacious homes ensconced in park-like settings.

Across the street stands the headquarters of the International Monetary Fund, the dogmatic dispenser of short-term monies for countries in financial straits. One of the least liked stops for Third World finance ministers, the IMF is nominally in the same business as the Bank—promoting economic development in poor nations by offering loans and advice—but the two institutions are barely on speaking terms, and collaborative efforts run hot and cold.

The Bank's Power

Four hundred yards away is the White House, a symbol of the strongest nation on Earth. A large number of the Bank's members criticize U.S. policy, through their diplomats, U.N. votes, and other actions because the U.S. interferes in the internal affairs of poor countries. For the Bank, meddling in the economic affairs of borrower nations is second nature, yet it receives less disparagement. Within the institution, it is generally acknowledged that the economic policies of a least 30 countries are supervised by Bank employees, that these nations are dependent on a lifeline of continued Bank lending, and that their leaders have no practical recourse other than submission to Bank-instituted directives. One pitiful spectacle is Kenya, a poor African nation of 32 million people; one-half of the government's budget is supplied by bilateral and multilateral aid.

Perhaps more alarming is the number of failed World Bank projects where the debtor nation is stuck with the bill. A measure of the Bank's power is the near total silence of its member nations, particularly those that are heavy borrowers. This power is translated into fear and it produces a chilling effect on reform debates.

Why is the Bank so powerful? For starters, it is the largest development institution in the world. Its $230 billion loan portfolio touches over 120 poor nations. For a few dozen of these smaller borrowers, the Bank represents the major, and sometimes only, source of long-term foreign capital. Typically, these nations do not have access to commercial banks because of extreme poverty or a bad repayment record. Other development agencies mirror Bank loan policy, so its financing is magnified with additional monies. International commercial interests also see a Bank loan quite naively, in my opinion, as a "Good Housekeeping

Seal of Approval" for a nation's overall economic program, and the institution's imprimatur thus extends to private finance. Complementing this situation is the massive public relations budget and the expansive research department, which collectively serve to place its ideology at the forefront of developmental thought.

On this day in June, it is no surprise that developing countries treat World Bankers "in the field" like visiting royalty. These governments stage endless meetings for their benefit and accord them diplomatic perks. A complaint of Third World officials, and one whispered under their breath, is the arrogance and rigidness of Bank employees on these field trips. Over the years, staffers become insensitive to local conditions and downplay them in designing loans. This lofty attitude is not restricted to the field; the stiltedness and insensitivity remain a source of irritation within the Bank itself. Country program coordinators (or loan officers) routinely carry a professorial air and cut off colleagues making suggestions on less than complete knowledge. In one meeting regarding a loan to Venezuelan investment banks, I pointed out the large exposure that the government would incur if it absorbed 100% of the underwriting risk of corporate securities. The primitive state of Venezuela's financial markets, the speculative nature of securities trading there, and the lack of sophisticated investment analysis argued for a risk sharing mechanism between government and industry. I was the only one in the room with Wall Street experience, but my five trips to Venezuela did not qualify me as an "expert" according to the task manager, who quickly dismissed my insights. The unwillingness to consider third party input "in" and "out" of country places a wall between the staff and its clientele.

A Board Meeting

Upstairs, the Board Room hosts the regularly scheduled Directors meeting. Among other matters, today's agenda includes a $500 million loan to promote roads in Brazil, one of the Bank's largest borrowers with over $9 billion in loans outstanding. The loan is denominated in U.S. dollars, in spite of the fact that over 80 percent of the expenses of the project are in local currency. No one in the meeting questions why a U.S. dollar loan is made to finance expenses that are paid for in Brazilian funds. Brazil spends $10 billion per year on defense. No one asks if some of this defense money can be directed to roads so Brazil can lessen its reliance on foreign debt. Nothing is said about corruption in the Brazilian government, which will administer the loan and has scandals reaching into the president's inner circle. Of the hundreds of pages of material written to evaluate the project, only a few touch on the fact that Brazil has a rigid class structure, limiting hope of social mobility for the lower classes. Not one page outlines Brazil's plan, if any, to mobilize sufficient hard currency resources in the future to repay this loan, or any of its $9 billion in World Bank loans. Despite the numerous omissions, the loan is approved unanimously.

The Brazilian approval is far from atypical. The Board considers dozens of loans each year without asking such questions, and members have little desire to rectify the circular process of bad lending and bad borrowing. The lack of constructive participation has reached the point where Bank managers view the Board approval process as a formality, and individual Board members are considered a nuisance, since they only call managers to answer inane questions such as "Does the project create local jobs?" or respond to parochial concerns such as "Can foreign firms bid on the contract?" In the eyes of Bank personnel, the Board's role as a guiding force is nonexistent, and its inability to provide direction supports the notion that loan volume is more important than economic development. Regrettably, the Directors representing the five largest shareholders—the United States, Japan, Germany, France and England—remain divided on what represents proper policies, principles, and procedures. In their stead stands the World Bank's bureaucracy, 8,500 strong, and the poor governments that require a steady stream of cash.

Bank Origins

Few of the Bank's 38 founding members in 1945 thought that its post-war role would evolve into a perpetual loan machine. Chartered out of the rubble of World War II, the institution's modest mission was to assist in the reconstruction and economic development of its member countries. Capital from wealthy, developed nations was diverted to lesser developed countries in a constructive manner. Indeed, the first three loans were made in 1947 to France, the Netherlands, and Denmark, respectively, for rebuilding infrastructure damaged by the war. Ten years after its beginning, the Bank's loan portfolio totaled $2.8 billion among 40 of its 64 members. By 1967, membership had increased to 106 countries with outstanding loans of $12 billion. Over the next 40 years, the membership roll grew to 184 and loans rose by nearly 20 times to $230 billion.

Each member provides cash for the Bank's capital and pledges additional contributions in case of a Bank debt default. The top five stockholders—the United States, Japan, Germany, France and England—control 37 percent of the votes. With a paid-in equity of $12 billion and pledges of $178 billion, the International Bank for Reconstruction and Development, the World Bank's principal unit, has a AAA credit rating, and it borrows huge sums ($14 billion in new bonds in 2006) to finance its programs. The basic principle of lending is that the Bank borrows money cheaper than it relends it, thus making a small spread like a commercial bank. Its loans are quite advantageous to the borrowers, many of which cannot obtain money from normal market sources. The Bank offers lengthy repayment schedules, relieving recipients of short-term financial pressures and enabling them to consider investments with a long-term payoff.

The Bank's Services

The Bank does not provide the services associated with commercial banks. It does not carry checking accounts, savings accounts, or trust accounts for its members. Neither are foreign exchange, asset management or cash handling services offered. The primary product is the long-term loan, supplemented by economic advisory and technical engineering advice. In addition, the Bank has a large research department that, unlike a private bank, creates and publishes studies on subjects relevant to the development process.

The institution has been known as the World Bank for more than half a century despite the fact that many countries have not been represented during past years. Only in the 1990's did many of the former communist countries sign on. Fifteen of the former Soviet republics and satellites came aboard in 1992 and 1993. The "World" part of the name is almost a misnomer. About 40 percent of the loan portfolio is accounted for by just seven members: Bangladesh, Brazil, China, India, Indonesia, Mexico and Pakistan.

The membership is segmented into the wealthy "developed" countries and the poor "developing" countries. The former includes the

United States, Canada, Japan, most of the Western European nations and a number of other nations scattered around the globe. The developing label encompasses the majority of the membership, which is eligible for loans.

The Fundamental Paradox

The institution's purpose is to graduate the "poor members" into "rich status," but most of the borrowers remain in an impoverished state even after receiving billions in loans and advice. This is the paradox of the Bank's existence and the staff has never tried to disapprove it. Indeed, a seminal study by William Easterly, a Bank employee who is now a New York University professor, compared aid to borrower prosperity, and found no correlation. Evaluating the results of its loans is not one of the Bank's strong points, and such analysis is frowned upon by the higher ups. During one lunch conversation, one of my former colleagues, a World Bank middle manager, reflected on why more work was not dedicated to this effort, considering the amounts spent on studying other topics. She sat silently for a second. Turning her head to the right and to the left, she checked to see if anyone eavesdropped. Satisfied of confidentiality, she whispered, "Nobody likes talking about that around here."

As evidence of this state of affairs, one only need consult the 2006 annual report, which shows the relative pittance of $20 million, or one percent of a $2.2 billion operating budget, allocated to the Independent Evaluation Group (IEG), which measures the effectiveness of Bank loans. The comparable internal audit group of the U.S. Agency for International Development spends substantially more as a percentage. In contrast, the Bank's public relations department enjoys a budget four times the size of the IEG, and it is an extraordinary tub thumper for the Bank's activities. Hundreds of magazines, books, studies, seminars, references, and press releases describe Bank projects as remarkable examples of innovation, and the commercial media succumbs to the relentless onslaught of propaganda.

Despite the imagery, making loans, not solving development problems, is the name of the game. Besides, most Bank managers, frustrated at their clients' lack of progress, believe the problems of poor countries are too intractable to be solved with simple finance packages. This sentiment, born out of 15 or 20 years at the institution, is well founded, but it creates a large class of careerists, who have given up any youthful pretension of "making a difference."

The Brazilian Approval

Today, on this day in June, the Board approves the Brazilian road project, among other matters. Such meetings are bland, purposeless affairs, staged to put the formal endorsement on loans that have received the nod from the senior executive corps. A minute after the meeting begins, Paul Wolfowitz walks into the Board room. The 24 executive directors, representing nations from all over the world, flank him on either side of a large table, with senior officers and alternate executive directors sitting beside them. Behind the table are rows of seats filled with managers, observers, and staffers. After a few words from Mr. Wolfowitz, Aymeric-Albin Meyer, team leader of the Brazilian project, takes 90 seconds to read the salient details of the project. In a monotone, clear enough to be picked up by the stenographers present, he recites its purpose, cost, and benefit from two typed pages. Accompanying him here are World Bank employees, Pamela Cox, vice president of the Latin America division, John Briscoe, Brazil country director, and Jose Luis Irigoyen, sector manager, who assist on two minor questions posed by Board members. The directors ratify the project and move on to the next loan.

As poor countries attempt to alleviate poverty, some find themselves in need of a fat bank account and serious technical advice. The Bank purports to provide both, but the persistence of grave problems within its client list raises two questions: One, are Bank loans developmental? And two, does its policy advice have value?

II.
THE WORLD BANK, ITS CLIENTS AND GLOBAL POVERTY

A Japanese banker, who had been placed with the Bank by his government, once told me, "The World Bank is the only bank in the world where no one knows anything about banking!" This statement is an apt portrayal of the contradictory aspects of development lending, which are illustrated in part by the Brazilian road project. An understanding of the institution and its relevance to global poverty begins with a brief description.

The World Bank Group

The World Bank Group consists of the International Bank for Reconstruction and Development (IBRD), the International Development Association (IDA), the International Finance Corporation (IFC), and the Multilateral Investment Guarantee Agency (MIGA). These organizations exist for one central purpose: to promote economic and social progress in poor developing nations. Although technically two separate corporations, the IBRD and IDA share employees and offices and are collectively referred to in this book as the "World Bank." The IFC and MIGA are smaller and operate with separate staffs. Controlling over $315 billion in assets and employing 10,000 people, the World Bank seeks to carry out its function in three ways: lend funds to countries on a concessionary basis; provide governments with technical advice on a variety of social and economic matters; and serve as a catalyst for private investment that would normally not consider the developing world. The Bank's lending program in 2006 was $21 billion, an amount equal to the combined foreign aid programs of England, France and Germany.

The Bank is owned by 184 member countries and only a few countries have chosen not to become members. The United States is the largest shareholder with 16% and 13% of the shares of IBRD and IDA, respectively, but the Bank is not legally controlled by the U.S. or any other sovereign government. Its business is conducted autonomously under the supervision of a multilateral board of directors, and each employee is accorded the same diplomatic status as a United Nations employee. This arrangement aims to reduce the influence of political officials of member governments on Bank staff.

The IBRD is the oldest and largest of the four Bank institutions. It was founded in 1945, under the spirit of post-World War II international cooperation that also created the United Nations. Both the IBRD and the IDA, formed in 1960, provide loans strictly to governments while the IFC, established in 1956, invests in private businesses in developing countries. MIGA, formed in 1988, sells insurance to cover political risks in developing country investment.

Most of the money the World Bank lends comes from its own borrowings in the international capital markets, where, by virtue of the guarantees of its large creditworthy members, it enjoys a AAA bond rating. Other funds come from members' contributions and from repayments on past loans. Like commercial banks, the Bank makes a profit by charging borrowers interest rates that are higher than its own cost of funds. This spread covers its cost of doing business and provides a small return to shareholders as a bonus.

Developing Countries Defined

The World Bank's clients are poor countries with per capita incomes of less than $9,400. Over 150 nations fit this definition, encompassing 80 percent of the world's population and 75 percent of sovereign states. Most have per capita incomes of less than $3,000, which translates into an average household income of $4,000. This small amount supports four people on about $3 per person per day. Other labels for these countries include developing countries, emerging markets, low-income countries, and the Third World. By way of comparison, the United States has a per capita income of $37,600, and a median household income of $47,000. On the basis of their economic size alone, the emerging markets are not a major force, representing a combined 20 percent of global gross national income (GNI). The largest three emerging economies—China, Brazil, and Russia—provide just seven percent of global GNI. In contrast, the top three developed countries—the United States, Japan, and Germany—contribute 51 percent.

The words "developing country" and "developed country" do not do justice to the dramatic differences between the two classes of economy. For people who have not traveled extensively, it is difficult to visualize the grinding poverty afflicting most developing countries. Things most of us take for granted in the United States—a telephone, a decent home, and a family car—are not within the means of the average breadwinner. Well-paying jobs are scarce and advancement opportunities are limited, as wealth is concentrated in the hands of a small elite who promote a rigid class structure. The sharp differences are described by Eduardo Doryan, former vice president of human development for the Bank. The problem in places such as India, "is that you'll see at least two countries, one where most people are on a boat heading back to the nineteenth century and another where the boat is heading to the twenty-first."

Are Developing Countries Important?

In contrast to their small income contribution, the developing countries attract considerable attention from the West. Certain poor nations sit astride important shipping lanes and sensitive border areas. Several have large armies and substantial arsenals that, when combined with a lack of political stability and recurrent xenophobia, present the wealthier countries with spill-over problems that they prefer to avoid. For this reason, the West put substantial resources into resolving problems with Iraq, Iran, North Korea, Bosnia, Sudan, the Congo, and other nations.

Developing countries supply many of the materials necessary to keep the industrialized economies running. Nigeria, Mexico, Venezuela, Indonesia, and several Middle Eastern countries are major sources of oil—still the most vital energy source of the First World. Similarly, Papua New Guinea, Jamaica, Brazil, Russia, and China supply half of the world's aluminum ore, and emerging markets provide most of the production of other key minerals such as copper, tin, iron, manganese, and chromium. If the flow of these resources were to be cut off for only a few months, the wealthy economies would experience severe dislocations, if not unbridled panic.

In addition to natural resources, the Third World is a low-cost labor source. Multinational corporations transfer production plants from developed locations to these areas, and save on costs. If this practice were stopped, the expense of making goods domestically would increase Western living costs, while Third World poverty would increase. Millions of developing country residents immigrate, legally and illegally, to the wealthy nations each year. For the most part, these immigrants work at the low end of the wage scale, which, nevertheless, is higher than comparable pay in their home countries. By way of example, the United States has 12 million illegal immigrants, equal to one ninth of Mexico's population.

The dynamics of the poor nations supplying the Western countries, as opposed to buying Western goods, are illustrated in Exhibit 2.1, which shows the trade surpluses enjoyed by developing nations against the United States. Malaysia, for example, sold $33 billion worth of goods to the United States in 2005, yet imported only $10 billion. Over the long term, the United States and other developed nations expect the trade deficits to moderate, as the Third World grows out of its supplier role and becomes a larger consumer of Western goods. Although the potential is there, the progress will come in fits and starts. Even at a continuous high rate of growth, say six percent, it takes a relatively prosperous country, like Venezuela, 60 years to reach the level of the United States.

Exhibit 2.1 2005 Balance of Trade Surplus with U.S., Principal Emerging Market Trading Partners (in Billions)

China	$202
Mexico	50
Venezuela	28
Malaysia	23
Nigeria	23
Thailand	13
Russia	11
India	10
Brazil	9
Indonesia	8

Source: U.S. Census Bureau Merchandise Trade Report.

The World Bank describes the better-off members of the developing world as upper-middle-income, with annual per capita GNI of $3,000 to $9,400. The middle-income category has GNI of $725 to $3,000 per capita, and the low-income countries fall under $725. The population in each grouping is shown in Exhibit 2.2. Most residents of "low-income" nations operate on a subsistence level and lack access to modern requirements, such as portable water, electricity, schooling, and health care.

Exhibit 2.2   Poor Countries by Income Category

	Population (Millions)
Upper middle income	335
Middle income	2,655
Low income	2,310
Total	5,300

Source: World Bank Atlas 2004

Brief History

The history of developing nations mixing with the First World dates back centuries. Long-distance trade can be traced to Marco Polo, but sustained entries started around 1500 when Europeans established navigable sea routes around South Africa and across the Atlantic to North and South America. Holland and England made significant inroads into Asia in the sixteenth century, and England and France colonized several fronts in North America. By the mid 1700s, large portions of what we now call the emerging markets were controlled by the European powers. By the mid 1800s, independence movements decolonized most of the Americas, and the European powers focused their efforts on previously unexplored areas of Africa. By 1900, Africa was effectively administered by European nations.

The 1900s saw the colonial system disintegrate. The cost of defending their rules became too costly for the European states, and revolutions and nationalistic movements put pressure on the powers to disband their empires. Today, the traditional colony has effectively disappeared, although poor countries complain that neo-colonialism has taken its place. They view themselves as politically independent, but their ability to control their own destiny is compromised and constrained by the actions of Western states, transnational corporations, and international financial agencies.

Recognize the Differences

Even as more than 150 countries fold into one group, note these nations are extremely diverse, not only among economic lines, but also among historical, cultural, political, and religious attributes.

For example, the principal income marker—below $9,400 per capita—covers a wide range of circumstances. At the high end is Barbados. A popular tourist destination, it has attractive offices, apartments and hotels, and the roads are paved and filled with cars. The people are well-fed, well-dressed, and well-equipped with modern conveniences. At the bottom of the range lies Somalia. The main cities are ramshackle affairs, with crumbling office buildings and pot-holed streets. Electricity reaches a small minority of homes for several hours a day. The few cars on the road are beaten-up jalopies that share passage with pedestrians, bicycles, farm animals, and horse-drawn wagons. Healthcare, schooling, and related government services are meager to non-existent, and the majority of the populace is tied to the land, living a lifestyle that is a throwback to medieval times.

With vast segments of the population involved in agriculture, the typical developing country has a small industrial base relative to a rich nation. Wealthy groups control the principal components of industrial activity, and with their political and economic influence, they restrain new domestic and foreign competitors. By way of illustration, even after 13 years of NAFTA, Mexico has duopolies in television, telecom, beer, tobacco, soda, bread, and cement. Pricing is higher than would be the case with competition, so the poor pay more.

Politics and Government

Only a handful of the developing countries approach the freedom and openness of the U.S. and Western European democracies. On the other hand, most are not oppressive military dictatorships, so the vast majority fit somewhere in between. Many make transitions to multiparty democratic rule. Even in the quasi-democracies, freedom of the press is restricted, and one can hardly pick up a *New York Times, Washington Post,* or *Wall Street Journal* without seeing an emerging market government harass a media outlet that becomes too critical of the ruling class.

The tradition of public service is not well established in the Third World. Too many politicians and civil servants in poor countries view a government career as akin to a private sector job, with one primary goal in mind—making money. Since public sector jobs have low salaries—as compared to a private position—the difference is made up, unfortunately, by bribes and insider deals. In one illustration, China's National Audit Office estimated the annual loss from corruption at 14 percent of national income. Many individuals who reach the upper pinnacles of developing country administrations amass huge fortunes—with no questions asked. Carlos "Hank" Rhon worked in several Mexican administrations, never earning more than $200,000 per year, yet Forbes magazine placed his net worth at $1 billion. Mr. Rhon coined the phrase, "a politician who is poor is a poor politician."

Currency and Financial Markets

A nation's currency is a proxy for its financial and political stability. For example, the world's strongest currency, the Swiss Franc, is administered by Switzerland. It has had the same representative democracy for 168 years, and its government finances are beyond reproach. These dual qualities made the country—and its currency—a haven for millions of investors over the years, and Switzerland is a mega banking center, despite the country's small population.

The U.S. dollar ranks high everywhere as a solid currency. Although it has depreciated over the years relative to the Swiss franc, the dollar is a mainstay of international commerce, due largely to the size of the U.S. economy. Broad-based commodities such as oil and paper are priced in dollars, and many international transactions, irrespective of location, are priced or indexed to the dollar. This custom includes the business sector, as well as the man on the street. In every poor country that I visit, the dollar is a de facto substitute currency. People accept dollars for routine purchases such as taxi rides and meals.

The desire for U.S. money rather than the local currency is the product of common sense. History illustrates that developing country currencies do not hold their value. People living there know this fact and they act accordingly. Low-income nations' residents hoard U.S. dollars and accumulate hard assets that retain value, such as gold jewelry. In Russia, for example, the government acknowledges a large part of domestic savings is not invested locally; rather, it is tucked away in large U.S. bills in mattresses and deposit boxes. Rich families maintain offshore accounts that are invested in Western financial markets, as well as "round trip" commitments to local businesses. The latter is evident in the Korean convertible bond market, where most deals are underwritten by Swiss banks, major repositories for Korean "flight capital." Exhibit 2.3 illustrates how currencies have devalued by 50 percent and more.

Exhibit 2.3 Currency Value Depreciation (in Percent) Against U.S. Dollar, 1986-2006

	Last 20 Years (%)
Asia	
Chinese yuan	56
Indian rupee	71
Indonesian rupiah	85
Latin America	
Argentine peso	94
Mexican peso	91
Europe	
Russian ruble	99
Polish zloty	99
Africa	
Egyptian pound	88
South African rand	65

Source: IMF Statistics

With neither locals nor foreigners having faith in a currency's forward worth, a poor nation's capital markets are short-term oriented. Investors do not want to lose money over the unpredictable long-term, so trading is dominated by three to six month financial instruments. The rare long-term debt issue has a floating rate designed to insulate the holder against changing interest levels. For example, the longest fixed-rate bond available in Brazil, a major emerging market, is nine months. The lack of a bond market has repercussions for the average breadwinner. Since lenders are reluctant to commit on a long-term basis, there are no 20-year mortgages available for wage earners. The prospective homeowner must come up with substantial cash, like fifty percent of a home's purchase price, or he is consigned to renting. Home ownership promotes stability in society and a belief that the owner has a stake in his country's future.

Without it, poor countries face problems in getting citizens to buy into the system.

Stock markets are speculative in nature. Investors cannot rely on the Warren Buffet style of studying a security and holding it for the long haul; it is too easy for country crises to overwhelm an individual company. Furthermore, accounting is suspect and stock exchanges are lax in enforcing the rules. Even with careful analysis, an investor relies on educated guesswork. More often than not, people bet wildly, giving the stock markets a casino mentality. In the space of one year, huge trading swings can take place. In 2006, for example, Indonesia's stock market climbed 25 percent, fell 15 percent, and then rose 29 percent. With the stock market viewed as a game of chance, local investors are reluctant to commit large sums to equities. Entrepreneurs are stymied and innovation is attenuated.

Social Organization

North America and Western Europe have a high percentage of people who are "middle class." They live in comfortable economic surroundings—including a modern home, car, and similar conveniences—and hold jobs paying salaries that exceed the cost of the basic necessities. In the United States, the definition of middle class covers over 80 percent of the population. In Germany, this percentage exceeds 90 percent. A large middle class is conducive to social stability and participatory democracy.

The level of material possessions for a middle-class family in an emerging market is substantially less than the United States or Germany; however, the basic thrust is the same. The middle-class is an anchor for stability, even in a poor society. Unfortunately, low-income countries do not have a sizable middle class. As noted earlier, they are characterized by a small group of elite families enjoying tremendous wealth, and a vast underclass living hand to mouth. Consider Brazil, Latin America's most populous nation. Three percent of the population owns two-thirds of the land. One Peruvian described Latin America as follows: "We're essentially a feudal society. There are two classes: nobility and peasant. There's little upward mobility, so we don't have a middle class. Rights and privileges pass through the traditional wealthy families."

Besides a rigid class structure, these societies confront other obstacles, including racism, tribalism, sexism, and religious discrimination. These forces are more pronounced in developing countries than in rich nations. A key function of local armies is simply to maintain order among the factions. The spread of Western culture, which increasingly promotes equality and tolerance, weakens these forces, but modernization takes time.

Foreign Aid and The Costs of Global Poverty

The challenges of these developing countries are many, and Western governments provide direct foreign aid of about $80 billion annually. An important part of their poverty relief is delegated to the Bank and its regional offspring (i.e., the Inter-American Development Bank, the Asian Development Bank, the European Bank for Reconstruction and Development, and the African Development Bank). Collectively these five institutions loan over $35 billion annually. In connection with the financing, these organizations provide advice to borrowers on a wide range of topics. Despite the massive injection of money and advice into poor countries, the development banks and foreign aid grants are ineffective. Billions of people live at subsistence levels, and the Third World remains dominated by backward economies, corrupt governments and statist systems.

The cost of poverty involves huge expenditures for the West with respect to terrorism, instability, and illegal immigration. With little hope of improvement, poor people left behind can turn into radicals, directing their frustrations at the prosperous nations. In the U.S., for example, the government budget for homeland security exceeds $40 billion annually. These amounts exclude the expense of related military and intelligence work, as well as taxpayer time and inconvenience at airports, border crossings, and secure buildings. If one reasonably presumes a $10 per barrel "instability tax" on shaky oil supplies from the Third World, poverty costs increase another $100 billion annually. To these amounts can be added the West's cost of trying to fix failed states, such as Afghanistan.

Seeking opportunity, millions immigrate illegally to the United States and Western Europe. They come by desert trails, ship-borne containers, and rickety boats, originating from the teeming slums of Mexico, Brazil, China, and similar countries. Patrolling borders, providing social services to illegal immigrants, and enforcing applicable laws represent sizeable outlays for Western governments. If their home countries were functioning properly, these immigrants might choose to stay put.

Connecting the Bank to Global Poverty

A portion of these costs lies at the feet of the World Bank, which has assumed the mantle of the preeminent development institution. To a poor country in a financial crisis, the organization is a "sugar daddy," providing long-term loans and offering policy advice. In taking such advice, Third World leaders view the Bank as a Western institution, and some naively think they receive policies that are proven successes. Some leaders think it knows "how to get development done," but the truth is the Bank does not know. Its policies are wrong and its loans simply put the recipient in deeper debt.

Even for those poor countries that are not in crisis, the Bank remains an insidious influence. It says it is the "Knowledge Bank" for development and pushes its intellectual framework for economic progress. Countries that do not subscribe to the framework lose the stamp of approval conferred by the Bank and the International Monetary Fund (IMF), making it almost impossible for those nations to attract Western loans and investments. The influence of the Bank and its offspring, therefore, extends far beyond their stream of loans. It involves a host of low-income nations following a range of Bank-mandated policies that separate them from the Western matrix of wealth and progress, and place them on a path toward sustained poverty and chaos. In the end, the West's principal enemy is neither a religion nor a country, but a condition in which a large portion of the planet's population functions without hope.

The U.S. is the Prime Enabler

The United States is the prime enabler behind the World Bank's ineffectiveness. It is the principal guarantor of the $160 billion in bonds issued by the Bank, without which the organization could not fund its lending operation, and it provides about one billion in cash payments annually to subsidize Bank initiatives. As the largest stockholder, the U.S. appoints both the Bank president and a permanent executive director, neither of whom stress accountability or alter the status quo. The U.S. must do better.

In fairness, the U.S. extracts short-term benefits from the institution. As the largest shareholder, it receives partial credit for the aid extended to recipients, and this assistance is often granted to coincide with foreign trips by U.S. delegations. To a limited extent, the U.S. pushes Bank loans to favored allies, such as Pakistan, where direct funding by the U.S. may result in accusations of American domination by local political actors. Further, the Bank's current ideology emphasizes democracy, privatization, and anti-corruption, all causes that the U.S. espouses with varying degrees of intensity. On a provincial level, the Bank, the IFC and MIGA account for 10,000 highly-paid jobs in the Metro Washington area and pump additional cash into the region through contractors.

An unspoken rule at the Bank is that the U.S., the largest shareholder, nominates the Bank president. Upon the retirement of Jim Wolfensohn in 2005, President George W. Bush nominated Paul Wolfowitz, then the deputy secretary of defense and well known for his controversial role in the Iraq War. As soon as the nomination was announced, the Bank and its lobbying machine went into motion. Suspicious of Republican policies, the senior staff wanted to put the Bush administration on the defensive, to kill any inkling of reform, and to transform Wolfowitz from an independent thinker into a Bank cheerleader, powerless to fight the bureaucracy. In responding to critics, Wolfowitz deflected opposition with conciliatory statements, but his appeasement is contrary to Western interests in fixing poverty problems.

Operating with impunity but without accountability, the World Bank has transformed its charter into an environment where results do not matter. The institution needs a dramatic overhaul. In France, *Le Monde* called the Wolfowitz nomination "an indifference or even cynicism towards poor countries." This is untrue. The worst indifference is in the Bank itself. Frustrated by its inability to conquer poverty, it has given up searching for real solutions in favor of preserving its privileges.

III.
TODAY'S PROBLEMS

In a July 31, 2006 speech before the Heritage Foundation, a Washington think tank with key ties to the Republican leadership, World Bank President Paul Wolfowitz lost an opportunity to promote a vision. Rather than lash out at small minds who stymie reform, he recited shopworn platitudes about development progress, good governance, and Third World entrepreneurship. After 16 months at the helm, he should have realized that the Bank's problems need a broad public hearing.

Limited Resources

First and foremost are the Bank's limited resources in the face of an expansive policy agenda. In 2006, it lent $21 billion to Third World governments, but collected $15 billion in loan repayments, indicating a net outflow of $6 billion. This largesse is allocated to over 100 countries with five billion people, so the fiscal impact is small, only $1.20 per person per year. The net outflows are decreasing, as members attract commercial loans, use export revenues, and receive immigrant remittances. A similar situation exists with foreign aid, which comes in such forms as official government to government grants, other multilateral loans, bilateral loans, and charitable contributions (from Western individuals and foundations to poor countries). In 2006, the Bank's net outflow was less than ten percent of total global foreign aid, and that percentage has been declining for years.

In those seven countries where forty percent of its loans are concentrated, the Bank represents a miniscule amount of total foreign investment, and its continued involvement in large economies such as Brazil, China, and Mexico is an inappropriate use of resources. How does management justify its $180 million loan in September 2006 to China, which received $70 billion in foreign direct investment in that year and had $1 trillion in foreign currency reserves? Even if you assume that the copycat institutions mirror the Banks' policies exactly, its impact remains small.

At the same time as its financial importance diminishes, the Bank broadens its agenda. It aims to tackle poverty, environment, health, education, infrastructure, governance, and private sector issues for 100 plus clients simultaneously. The result: development money and staff are spread thin, and nothing lasting is accomplished. The political and economic systems of many recipient countries have overwhelming problems, and the amount of foreign aid is marginal relative to the size of their economies. Most of it does not prepare the recipient to be self-sufficient, and the Bank has yet to come to grips with that reality. Perhaps the policies and prescriptions might work if the institution acknowledged its limitations and structured its projects accordingly. Penn professor Devesh Kapur summarized the ability to effect change:

> Relentless pressure on the Bank, however, obscures another reality: the Bank is a small actor whose global efforts for the most part have been dwarfed by much more powerful forces, the sheer scale of demographic pressures, the rising material aspirations of billions of people, the information revolution, external shocks both political and economic, and technological change. It has rarely accounted in the aggregate for more than two percent of investment in LDC's (developing countries). The physical and human costs of poor national policies, poor investments, poor national leadership, and the meddling of the superpowers have vastly exceeded the worst efforts of the Bank.

Many Rulers Don't Want Development Programs

It is my belief that many Third World leaders do not want development. The tiny part of the population that controls industry and politics does very well financially, and economic progress in the form of Western ideals, competitors, and technologies can upset the applecart, even if it improves the lot of the vast majority. In the near term, external actors such as the Bank and the U.S. can do little to reverse this situation. Since the 1980's, the Bank has tried to link a large portion of its loan programs to recipients accepting technical advice and policy change. However, absent withholding further aid, the institution has relatively little power to force borrowers to implement its recommendations. In comparison, the U.S.'s new Millennium Challenge Corporation provides money to countries that show evidence of a real desire to reform. However, the few developing nations that fit this characterization limit such grants.

Wealthy Nations Not Firmly Committed

The preponderance of World Bank loans are "off-budget" items for the Bank's wealthy members, because the institution generates the requisite funds by selling bonds in the international capital markets. These members guarantee the bonds through obligatory capital calls, but such guarantees are off-budget until exercised. From their perspective, therefore, Bank money is free foreign aid, for which they are more than willing to take credit.

Outside of their involvement in the multilateral banks and the United Nations, most wealthy countries operate their own foreign aid programs, which are "on budget." In recent years, such programs represent about one percent of government spending. Some anti-poverty activists insist the rich nations can afford more and complain that their existing programs are tied to provincial interests, rather than true poverty alleviation. At the Monterrey Development Conference in 2003, rich countries pledged to increase aid substantially by 2015, but limited actions to date leave doubts about these pledges being met. Of course, as the Bank's own experience demonstrates, throwing money at problems does not solve them. In fact, some theorists encourage wealthy countries to cut aid in favor of reducing their agricultural subsidies and lowering their trade barriers. Such actions would allow Third World farmers to gain greater access to Western markets, promoting permanent growth.

The End of the Cold War

When the U.S. was locked in a bitter struggle with communism, the Bank's failures were excused by larger stockholders, in part, because the institution provided resources to poor countries siding with the West. After the fall of the Berlin Wall and the break-up of the Soviet Union, this rationale, and the lending program, lost relevance. With the institution having a finite supply of money, it is now reasonable to expect the Bank to show concrete results from its actions.

Clients' Access to Commercial Loans

In past years, the Bank rightfully claimed that clients were shut off from long-term debt markets. Its loans, and those of similar development banks, were thus stable funding sources that allowed low-income nations to match appropriately long-term projects with long-term capital. That is no longer the case.

The heightened interest in emerging market securities, the rise of international investment funds and the improvement in developing country finances have paved the way for large numbers of recipients to incur borrowings from private sources. Studies by Adam Lerrick of Carnegie Mellon University indicate that over 90 percent of the Bank's lending from 2001-2005 went to borrowers with bond ratings of B or higher, levels at which long-term U.S. dollar financing can be secured commercially. Twenty-five percent of loans were to investment-grade-rated nations, which can sell bonds at interest rates comparable to those of top U.S. corporations. For those countries without bond ratings, the commercial loan window is still open. Hedge funds lend long-term money to less credit worthy nations, such as Sudan and Tanzania, when "the transactions are structured properly," says Sanjeev Kumar, director of the Delamore Funds, a $5 billion investment manager. Thus, a substantial portion of the Bank's clients can find their own debt finance, and this fact undermines the justification for a large lending program. The institution now supplants private capital.

Continued Lack of Evaluation System

After 60 years in the development business, the Bank's economists have been unable to devise a system that evaluates quantitatively the merits of differing projects. This problem means that the Bank cannot compare scientifically the benefits of a $100 million hospital to a $100 million road to a $100 million privatization program, despite the fact that there are large variations in the returns of such projects. In other words, staffers "fly blind" when presenting the project values to Board members as well as to member governments. Choices are left to educated guesswork and political whimsy. This issue received traction when then World Bank Chief Economist Larry Summers featured it in a 1992 article, and it is the subject of on-again, off-again seminars and studies, such as the June 2003 data and statistics conference organized by the Bank and U.N. Development Program. But there is little sense of urgency.

An appropriate statistic for comparing development projects is the economic rate of return (ERR). An ERR is the economist's attempt to parallel the internal rate of return (IRR) calculation used in private business. For example, a major food company like Proctor & Gamble has a limited amount of money so it must choose its investments wisely. To allocate its capital each year, it selects those projects that offer the most attractive IRR's relative to their implied risk parameters. For example P&G might choose a factory expansion with a 20% return, over a brand extension campaign with a 15% return. For P&G, the IRR is a rational tool for allocating capital, and one that the World Bank should endeavor to copy.

In a selection of projects approved in 2006, less than 20 percent included a numerical rate of return, compared to 38 percent of projects utilizing ERR's 15 years ago. This is a regrettable change of course that inflicts great uncertainty into the decision process. In part, the decline in ERR use stems from the Bank's increasing support of projects whose benefits are hard to measure. Health programs are worthy endeavors, but the economic value of lives saved is difficult to quantify, as contrasted with the monetary worth of electricity supplied by a power plant. As the institution broadens health, social, education, environment, and other hard-to-measure projects, measurements of its effectiveness become more subjective and anecdotal than in the past. If Bank assistance was in the form of grants, this trend would be less disturbing, but the aid is in the form of US $-denominated loans that carry a repayment obligation. When a project fails to produce a significant benefit to the borrower, that country is saddled with both a dud project and a hefty financial obligation.

The difficulties in determining ERR's are less challenging today than they were 15 years ago. Computer modeling eases the calculation for such factors as the number of sick days avoided by quality health care, the transport hours saved by road maintenance, or the income increases provided by primary education. Unfortunately, the World Bank's Board does not demand this information, and the Bank's economists don't volunteer it. For the majority of projects that don't have ERR's, the organization relies on input-derived grading systems, surveys, or anecdotal evidence. For example, it might consider an education project successful because the 30 schools described in the loan documentation were constructed and the loan money was spent. However, the mere existence of the schools doesn't necessarily indicate that people were educated. That process depends on teachers showing up, textbooks being delivered, school maintenance being kept up and students being tested. Sometimes, the Bank administers a survey to project participants, asking them to indicate whether the project accomplished its objectives. Even if a majority responds "yes," that is hardly a scientific analysis of a project's returns. In other evaluation reports, the success definition is so dependent on multiple variables that the Bank's money can be tied, or not tied, to a given result, given a reviewer's inclinations.

No Accountability at the Bank

The lack of a reliable statistical measurement system leads some insiders to say that the World Bank has no "bottom line." Accomplishment is defined as the amount and number of loans handed out, rather than the quality and results of the loans. Furthermore, in the vast majority of cases, the borrower services the loan, whether or not the related project worked. This convention places the Bank's debt at a priority to a nation's commercial creditors, and it relieves the institution, for the most part, of financial penalties for failed projects.

For example, when Argentina defaulted on its sovereign obligations in 2001, its Government embarked on a long and tortuous restructuring process. Commercial creditors, such as bondholders and money-center banks, agreed to reduce the principal amount of their debts by 70 percent , thus incurring tens of billions in losses. Multilateral lenders, such as the Bank and IMF, accepted no discounts based on their traditional preferred positions.

Even if repayment risks are virtually non-existent, an executive should suffer career-wise if loans he initiated failed to meet objectives. However, the modest evaluation systems in place usually don't register for five to seven years after a loan closing. At that point, the executive has moved on to other positions and escaped blame for his actions. The ability to lend without the potential for dire consequences fosters a non-accountability culture. This result is bad for any financial firm, but unlike many lenders, the cost of the Bank's mistakes are born by the world's poorest nations.

Move-the-Money Syndrome

The lack of a measurement system and the avoidance of non-payment risk mean that the Bank's principal achievement is loan volume. Department heads receive a loan budget at the beginning of the fiscal year, and their responsibility is to make sufficient loans by year end to meet budget. The pressure to lend is constant, is disruptive of quality control, and is most evident at the end of the fiscal year, when the staff, in an attempt to hit targets, floods the Board with loan requests. In June 2006, the fiscal year's final month, for example, the Board ratified 65 loans, about one-fourth of the yearly total. In addition to the annual bunching, the move-the-money syndrome is evident in the Bank's reports, publications, and press releases. These documents tout loan approvals and loan volumes but pay short shrift to tangible results. The message comes through to staff members and borrowers alike.

The Bank Does Not Know What Works

Despite its air of professorial expertise, the Bank has little knowledge of how poverty is systematically eliminated in a given country. Through its history, the institution has lurched from one over-riding theme to another. Infrastructure, export substitution, social borrowing, structural adjustment, privatization, and the development plan known as the "Washington consensus" were governing principals that cycled through the organization, only to be rejected when they failed to produce results after billions of dollars of loans.

Part of the thematic change derives from the Bank learning from its mistakes, but other aspects reflect the institution adapting to its critics, whose theories may be equally flawed. The shifting focus indicates a lack of confidence in the institution's home-grown policy base, which more often than not, is either educated guesswork or the latest fashion statement, rather than a viable framework. In fairness, the Bank argues that its policies and projects are sound, but that their effectiveness is overcome by a borrower's political considerations, macroeconomic problems, and external shocks. In other words, "It's not our fault." However, these problems are part and parcel of a poor nation's existence. If a project cannot withstand a moderate degree of these exposures and be effective, the Bank can't contribute meaningfully to poverty alleviation.

Corruption

The corruption associated with the institution is both the ordinary variety, which is not aggressively sought out, and the indirect variety, which is related to projects designed to help rich people.

Ordinary corruption refers to instances where a portion of the funds disbursed from Bank loans are diverted through machinations of borrowing country officials and local and international contractors. Research devised by such divergent sources as Northwestern professor Jeffrey Winters; the 2004 U.S. Senate hearings on MDB corruption; *Business Week*; and the Bank's Indonesian staff suggest that fraud on World Bank projects amounted to as much as 30 percent. The methods by which "leakage" is accomplished are many and varied. Examples include a contractor using sub-standard construction materials in infrastructure, a procurement official receiving a kickback for awarding a Bank-funded contract, and a government minister funneling loan proceeds through a dummy consulting firm. The Bank takes steps to detect and mitigate corruption risks, but a serious reduction requires changes in the way of doing business.

In Transparency International's annual index of perceived corruption in a country, 70 emerging markets scored three or less, indicating severe corruption and most of the remainder scored five or less, indicating serious corruption. A web of graft links government, business, and organized crime in many emerging markets, and the Bank is passive in making real inroads to cut leakage. Sola Adeyeye, a member of Nigeria's national assembly, describes the problem in a 2006 *New York Times* article, "Greedy politicians are literally killing their own people by stealing the money for health care, for schools, for clean water, for everything the state should provide its people." Staffers are resigned to the problem and I have heard more than one say, "If we didn't loan to corrupt governments, we'd be out of business!" Obviously, the corruption game requires two to tango. Western contractors are active in illicit Third World dealings, and they have little to fear from their authorities. David Nussbaum, Transparency International's chief executive has noted, "It is hypocritical that OECD-based companies continue to bribe across the globe, while their governments pay lip-service to enforcing the law." Such is ordinary corruption.

The indirect version is equally damaging. The Bank works with the low-income nations' elite classes, which are often authoritative and skew the development process in their favor. Many staffers themselves are from prominent Third World families and some fail to condemn this approach. Other ill-designed projects receive approval through staff naiveté and ignorance. In 1997, the Bank approved a $90 million loan to Brazil for land reform. Poor people enlisted in the project, borrowed money and bought farm land. According to Flavia Barros, Sergio Saver and Stephen Schwartz, authors of "The Negative Impacts of World Bank Market-Based Land Reform," the large landowners controlling the supply of land offered the least productive land for sale, and the implementing Brazil agency (and the poor people) bought the unarable land at inflated prices with Bank money. Pakistan's irrigation network, a major Bank loan recipient, "has always served a privileged elite at the expense of the poor," noted Peter Bosshard and Shannon Lawrence of the Environmental Defense Fund.

Portfolio Performance

The Bank measures the performance of its own projects and refuses to allow outside evaluators to verify its self-grading. An in-house department, the Independent Evaluation Group, conducts performance reviews, although it can hardly be viewed as "independent." Dr. Vinod Thomas, the Group's director, has spent the last twenty years as a Bank professional, and his previous position was country director for Brazil. Like Dr. Thomas, the Group's permanent staff is comprised of long-time Bank employees. A number of the Group's reports are hard hitting in their criticism, but the fact remains that IEG professionals are unlikely to jeopardize their own careers, and those of their friends and colleagues, with consistently candid observations.

If the Bank itself declares that 25 percent of its projects, on average, do not succeed, it is reasonable to presume that a truly independent arbiter would uncover a higher rate, just as golfers exaggerate handicaps and gamblers underestimate losses. A 50 percent failure rate is realistic in my experience. Set against the difficult operating conditions in poor countries, the expansive agenda of many projects, and the reluctance of recipient governments to institute reforms, the statistic is unsurprising, but it provides an indictment of the Bank's operating model, and one that wealthy members should pay more attention to.

Out of Control Expenses

For an institution that gives advice to governments on budget management, the Bank pays little attention to its own expense structure. Administrative costs for 2006 totaled $2.2 billion, continuing their steady rise even as loan volume is flat. Perhaps one-third of this amount is dedicated to non-loan functions such as academic research, treasury work, and portfolio maintenance, so the Bank spends $1.5 billion annually to process just 279 projects, a cost of $5 million each.

The Staff

The existing senior staff may well represent the greatest liability. Deeply ingrained in the Bank's bureaucracy and totally accepting of its shortcomings, the senior staff has long since lost its sense of purpose. Maintaining the institution, rather than poverty alleviation, is the principal objective. The senior staff uses its influence over the poorest nations to quell dissent and exploits the lack of engagement by rich nations to muffle reforms. Highly resistant to change, they commit the Board to serving their own ambitions, which conflict with the organization's stated goals.

With few hard numbers from which to evaluate personnel, the senior staff makes the written word king at the Bank, and informs employees that report quality is of paramount importance. As a result, lower level staffers draft and redraft project memoranda 20 to 30 times. This wasteful and duplicative effort demonstrates the project leader's mastery of his subject, but it also enables internal reviewers to eliminate hints of controversy, unease or doubt that might be conveyed to an outside analyst. It is not surprising that most managers consider the memoranda describing a project to be more important to their careers than the project itself. Dissatisfaction with this situation is rife among junior personnel, but their grumblings never see the inside of the Board room.

The Staff Association is the collective employee voice in corporate policy, but it is of little help in remedying the endless wordsmithing. The bulk of its effort is diverting the Board from the occasional attempt to cut back on the permanent staff's expensive perks, which include lifetime job security, five weeks of vacation, free plane tickets for family trips home, free private school tuition for staff children, and, in many cases, free university tuition. The benefits extend from the lowliest-file clerk to the top Bank executive, and make the institution's overhead quite high compared to Western government financial agencies.

On top of these problems is the senior staff's inability to deliver reliable advice on market-based policies. Schooled in the Bank's traditional central planning mode, top management is unqualified to design and implement projects promoting the private sector. Virtually all senior executives, and the vast majority of middle-level managers, have never worked in business. They are uncomfortable with the unpredictability, irrationality and risk associated with free developed markets, let alone those associated with emerging markets. Most came to the World Bank directly out of graduate school, teaching or government and are untouched by the challenges of a corporation facing competition. Protected by the Bank's civil service system, where salaries only go up and jobs are secure, they have little personal experience with the profit-making function outside of a textbook. In sum, they have minimal practical experience with what Third World business people and multilateral corporate executives are talking about, and their skill set is more appropriate for a prior era, when market-based solutions ranked low on the development agenda.

On the occasions when I attended meetings involving World Bankers and private sector executives, it became painfully apparent that the Bank is far more interested in dealing abstractly with the private sector than actively engaging it. As an employee, I was amazed at the number of private-sector research papers and policy recommendations in which the authors failed to interview real business people. Why did this happen? Living, breathing corporate executives can, and do, contradict the staff's theoretical constructs, potentially throwing a project approval into jeopardy. Besides shunning executives for fear of refutation, the staff is simply ill at ease with the private sector. Style is a problem. Corporate executives have a tendency to be decisive, act on limited information, avoid extraneous paperwork and take chances. These characteristics are not shared by the Bank's bureaucrats, and the two sets of individuals mix like oil and water. Furthermore, the average professional distrusts businessmen. While there is substance to this suspicion, this does not mean that the executives' opinions are worthless or hopelessly out of touch in a developmental context.

Cleaning out large numbers of existing employees and bringing in new blood is the best answer to this situation. Therein lies the essential problem. The personnel system is steeped in the worst civil service tradition, making needed layoffs and demotions impossible; promotions are given routinely on the basis of seniority and one's success at organizational politics. When former president Jim Wolfensohn made a feeble attempt to weed out old-timers, he offered hundreds of millions in lucrative exit packages. The result: he replaced 25 year veterans with 15 year veterans, hardly a substantive difference. Secondly, an attempt at reform presupposes an attack on perverse employee incentives. Such an attack would break up the established norm and invite a diplomatic civil war, as aggrieved staffers employ their home embassies and borrower nations to make denigrating remarks about the proposed changes.

IV.
IT WAS DIFFERENT BACK THEN

In 1994, on the occasion of its fiftieth anniversary, the Board commissioned a book on the World Bank's history. Needing a trustworthy author to carry out this delicate task, the members turned to the Brookings Institution, the esteemed U.S. think tank located a few blocks away. In addition to considerable financial support for the project, the Bank offered Brookings almost unlimited access to the staff, an unusual action for the secretive multilateral, and it received significant amounts of research assistance, in the form of background information and statistical data, provided free of charge. Devesh Kapur, John Lewis, and Richard Webb, then three experienced authors, produced a monumental history of the Bank's first 50 years.

The Bank library has several copies available, sitting on a row of non-descript steel shelving. The book itself is massive, having 1,200 pages and weighing over four pounds. Infinitely detailed, verbose, and chock full of statistics, it is a metaphor for the ponderous manner in which the Bank conducts its own business. Tediously inching its way through policy, projects, and presidents, the book recounts the institution's history in punishing detail. The authors cast Bank deeds in a favorable light, but to management's chagrin, they were not 100 percent in favor of the organization's methods nor in total agreement with the staff's version of events. As a result, the public relations department directs newcomers looking for historical information to official sources rather than the Brookings book.

The Origins of the Bank

In July 1944, the United States and Great Britain met at Bretton Woods, a small community in New Hampshire, to organize a post World War II financial order. Out of this meeting grew the World Bank, an international cooperative venture designed to promote a noble, and optimistic, calling of apolitical reconstruction and economic development.

Little known today, however, is that the Bank's primary function, as envisioned by its creators, was to act as a catalyst for <u>private investment</u>. The provision of loans for social improvements and macroeconomic policy objectives, now the Bank's dominant function, was nowhere specified as its primary role.

Even in the institution's formative stages, the confusion over the Bank's true purpose was apparent. Should its activities be governed along the lines of a pure financial institution, such as a privately-owned commercial bank? Or, should its function be so important that the Bank by necessity would weigh constantly the political implications of its actions? The answers to these questions played out in the debate over the Bank's location. The backers for a commercial bank-like institution advocated a headquarters in New York, the world's financial center. Here, the staff could be drawn from the sophisticated financial firms already operating in the area. Equally relevant, Bank employees could benefit from close interaction with other finance professionals. Support for a Washington location, which implied a political slant to the fledgling operation, came mostly from Truman administration insiders who wanted the U.S. to keep a close rein on the Bank's activities.

The political insiders won the battle. Washington became the headquarters, and the institution was set-up just a few blocks from the White House. The United States was installed as the largest shareholder, subscribing to $3.2 billion of the Bank's capital of $7.7 billion, a huge sum at the time. The influence of the United States continued to be strong for the next fifteen years, so much so that, until the early 1960's, the development community often referred to it as the "American Bank," not only because of the U.S. impact on operating policy but also because half of the staff were American citizens.

Formal operations commenced in June 1946. By mid 1947, four loans had been approved. Proceeds assisted in the physical reconstructions of Denmark, France, Luxembourg, and the Netherlands, whose economies had been ravaged by the war. A short time later, in March 1948, the first development loan was made to Chile, a poor nation in need of basic infrastructure such as electric power facilities, roads and agricultural items. All loans were guaranteed by the respective borrowing governments. These five operations established a precedent that remained firmly embedded in the institutional psyche over the next 20 years: basic infrastructure loans are the most important.

The Catalytic Role

As set forth in the Bank's incorporation papers, loans were to place less emphasis on the provision of external funds to poor borrowers than on the performance of a catalytic role. The founders envisioned the Bank providing seed capital to investment-hungry, war-ravaged, and poverty-stricken nations, which would put the money to good use by furthering those development projects that attracted additional capital, both domestic and foreign, to the recipient country. Needless to say, the stated purpose of the Bank became open to various forms of interpretation and the institution had leeway to maintain itself. By the 1950's, for example, the staff characterized the Bank's project loans as "catalytic" with respect to generating private investment, although the scientific proof of this claim was in dispute.

Economic development was then equated with the expansion of a country's aggregate growth rate and most projects conformed to this objective. Brick and mortar projects constituted the overwhelming proportion of the Bank's loans and typically included electric power generating plants, roads, railroads, and telecom facilities. Public utility infrastructure projects were accepted as a precondition for development within the finance community, and their production rate or usage level could be quantitatively measured. Also, power plant construction, which comprised the largest category in terms of dollars lent during the first 15 years, required large amounts of foreign exchange for equipment and the Bank's intervention was thus doubly justifiable, since developing nations had foreign exchange shortages. Socially-oriented brick and mortar projects, such as hospitals, schools, and sanitation facilities, received minimal attention. Staffers recognized the need for this type of project, but the economic output of social loans was less measurable, and their development contribution stretched over a longer-term horizon, which suggested more uncertainty than standard projects. Vying for a conservative posture, the Bank avoided loans that were not developmental in the strictest sense.

Credit Standards

The preference for "hard" economic projects over "soft" social projects found support on Wall Street, where the "American Bank" raised most of its borrowed capital in the 1950's and 1960's. As a new financial institution, the Bank was eager to establish its own credit standing, apart from the formidable set of guarantees provided by its shareholders. At that time, junk bonds were avoided; U.S. bond investors were by and large a conservative lot. They insisted that the Bank's loan portfolio be held to a strict credit standard. The result was a straight-forward lending approach during the Bank's first two decades. The creditworthiness of a loan was thoroughly assessed on both the country level and the project level, and senior executives encouraged follow-up supervision by loan officers.

To illustrate, during the 1950's the Bank refused to lend to developing nations that were in arrears on any sovereign borrowing, and outstanding delinquencies with commercial lenders had to be settled prior to World Bank consideration of a loan. In this way, the Bank's own creditors were reassured of its lending standards, and they continued to buy its securities, providing the fuel for growth.

From these lending credit standards soon evolved a need for placing restrictive covenants in the project loans. Simply defined, restrictive loan covenants are the parts of a loan contract that prohibit the borrower from taking actions that damage the quality of the loan. For example, a typical covenant found in a commercial loan says that the company cannot borrow more than a predetermined amount of money. Once this debt level is exceeded, the lender has the right for immediate repayment. The thought is that once a certain amount of leverage is reached, the company no longer represents a "safe" borrower. Country loans and project loans involve restrictions with a different nature but the same objective—preserving the borrower's ability to repay the debt.

Conditions and Technical Assistance

Consider a loan to an electric utility to finance a new power plant. The electricity is sold to hundreds, perhaps thousands, of customers. A reasonable covenant for a lender to request in this case is that the utility charge sufficient prices for electricity in order for it to make a profit. To

American consumers, who are accustomed to investor-owned utilities, this covenant might seem nonsensical. In the Third World where the Bank operates, many governments own power and water utilities. Since the politicians don't want to stir unrest, they sometimes keep the rates for these critical services artificially low and, as a result, the utilities lose money. To ensure that its power projects were "economical" in the true sense of the word, the Bank imposed conditions on the borrower, such as a requirement for reasonable electricity rates. These conditions, or "conditionalities" as they were called, shifted over time from a means to achieve loan quality to an instrument for imposing the Bank's will on a grudging borrower's broad economic policies.

Even before the Bank attached strings to its loans, the staff realized that borrowers needed more than consultative advice on loans. By the early 1950's, lending policy was more or less established and finance proposals flowed regularly into headquarters. Most loan applications were poorly prepared and had little supporting documentation. Many were nothing more than hare-brained schemes to extract foreign exchange from the Bank. A large number of potential borrowers had neither the experience, nor the technical manpower, to prepare an acceptable proposal. Out of this need was created the Bank's Technical Services Department, eventually manned by a group of experts in fields as diverse as agriculture, population control, and steel making. The Department's initial mandate was to research a project and assist the borrower's civil servants in drafting a loan proposal. As the loan process evolved, this assistance turned into a takeover. By the 1970's, the borrower's civil servants stood by idly as the Bank's staff prepared the voluminous documents needed to satisfy the paper-hungry bureaucracy.

By 1966, twenty years after opening its doors, the Bank had compiled a solid record. Sticking with a hard lending approach, it had earned the development community's respect and had become the model for several regional multilaterals. Its membership roll had expanded, up to 96 from the original 38, and loan volume had risen steadily. The staff was a tightly knit group, numbering less than 1,500 and well thought of. The project success rate exceeded 90% and the Bank's securities had AAA ratings on Wall Street. The World Bank was on cruise control.

The Decline of the Locomotive Theory

The unfortunate truth was that small cracks started to appear in the Bank's carefully constructed façade. First, despite twenty years of being the leading development force, the Bank had not created a practical means of comparing the economic returns on differing projects—such as the return on a road versus the return on a dam. Second, the economies of certain borrowers expanded rapidly with the Bank's help, while the economies of others completely stalled. The Bank legions of economists had no coherent theory to explain this turn of events, except to say that the situation was complicated. A second generation of theorists began to attack the institution's fundamental lending principle, which placed a heavy reliance on the infrastructure "locomotive theory."

The theory suggested that capital was the main factor in development stimulation. Sizable investment in infrastructure, particularly energy and transportation, eliminated the bottlenecks that restricted economic industrial growth. Infrastructure investment served as an economic engine, pushing a nation's industrial base to a high level. As industrial activity expanded, the theory continued, national production and income grew. Practical experience indicated, however, that the infrastructure's benefits had a tendency to accrue to a few large corporations in the borrowing countries, a likely result given the fact that their economies were dominated by the state and a handful of family-run industrial groups. Over time, however, the theory insisted the accumulated wealth and job opportunities that came with infrastructure "trickled down" to society's poorer segments.

Unfortunately, the preponderance of benefits did not spread downward. In fact, there were worrisome signs that the same Bank policies that encouraged growth also promoted wealth concentration. In other words, the billions of dollars in loans enriched an already landed class. Irrigation projects benefited the large farm owners to the detriment of the subsistence farmers, and electric generation projects powered giant factories controlled by the rich families. Management devoted resources to studying the problem, but it did not push for a solution. The Bank was a conservative institution; the political and social aspects of income redistribution fell outside of its purview. As the 1960's unfolded, the acceptance of Great Society programs by the United States, the largest shareholder, influenced Bank personnel who believed that social problems contributed strongly to underdevelopment in the Third World. They aimed to characterize "social spending" as "development investment" and paid scant attention to the other major contributing factors, such as centrally planned economies that frustrated individual initiative and mercantile economies that perpetuated class divides.

The McNamara Reign

Enter Robert McNamara. He came to the World Bank presidency in 1968 after a controversial tour as U.S. defense secretary during the Vietnam War. An overseer of tens of billions of dollars of Pentagon spending, and an architect of the "guns and butter" fiscal strategy that put America into a spiral of budget deficits, McNamara seemed an unlikely candidate to run the World Bank. A successful Ford Motor executive prior to entering the Johnson administration, he had no experience as a banker and little foreign policy background. Yet, McNamara proved to be an extraordinary salesman for the Bank, and his success in expanding the institution went beyond every expectation, including his own. In 1968, for example, lending volume was $954 million, targeted for 62 projects. By McNamara's departure in 1981, thirteen years later, annual loan volume had increased more than 12 times, to $12.3 billion, covering 246 projects.

The employee count and operating budget rose enormously during McNamara's term. Upon his arrival, 1,600 people worked there and the annual operation budget totaled $38 million. At his departure, the employees ballooned to 5,800 and the budget exceeded $430 million. Membership had also broadened, from 98 countries in 1968 to 139 countries in 1981.

McNamara's vastly increased loan program had to be sold not only to the borrowers (i.e., the poor developing nations that were to repay the loans), but also to the large developed countries that supplied the Bank's equity capital, and to the international bond investors that purchased its securities. For the developed shareholders, he emphasized that higher loan volume was in their interests, for those amounts would come back to them once the recipient countries, newly flush with Bank money, imported machinery and equipment. Bond buyers received assurances that loans to developing countries had no risks. Bank lending had an excellent repayment record and there were no significant arrears.

A huge money train chugged into motion as the funding need grew. No longer was Wall Street the only market for the Bank's securities. McNamara saw that non-U.S. capital markets became important to the funding schemes. Before long, the institution was a regular borrower in the London and Tokyo capital markets and it visited other markets such as Germany and Switzerland. By the end of McNamara's reign, the Bank was the largest issuer of bonds in the world and a coveted client for the big investment banking houses of Wall Street.

McNamara's term left an indelible mark on the Bank, and old hands still marvel at the way he transformed the sleepy institution with the Foreign Service Club atmosphere into a financial behemoth with a Third World tinge. A key factor in McNamara's success was his reasonably young age at the time of his appointment. Unlike most bank presidents who have assumed their position in the twilight of their careers, McNamara was 51 years old in 1968. He was energetic and aggressive and prepared to fight the bureaucracy. His lack of banking experience had to be considered a plus in plotting a major expansion; he wasn't tied to the conservative lending philosophy that afflicted veteran employees and made them reluctant to rubber-stamp risky loans. Finally, for some reason unrelated to his monied background, McNamara had an almost missionary zeal toward alleviating global poverty, and he was willing to increase lending by billions to accomplish this goal.

Some of the new-fangled social lending did not sit well with established staffers, a number of them remnants of the British and French colonial services. They were aghast at the prospect of throwing money at Third World problems. No matter, hundreds of fresh young faces came to the fore. With these eager recruits, McNamara had a virtual army of loan officers ready to do his bidding and, clearly, his enthusiasm rubbed off on them. Years later, many of this vanguard rose to the top of the Bank bureaucracy. Forgetful, perhaps, of the Bank's original mission during their day-to-day paper shuffling, they spoke wistfully of the McNamara years. "We were crusaders with the wisdom of God behind us and the money to back it up. It was all magic, full of idealism and dreaming," said Kim Jaycox, then vice president of the African Department, at a 1992 gathering of McNamara alumni. "We concentrated on our quest for solutions with a passion I had never before seen at the Bank." Speaking of the first years of McNamara's term, Tony Churchill, then director of the Industry and Energy Department added, "There were so few of us (at first). We were young, bright-eyed and bushy-tailed, and full of energy. We even looked different from the average, more conservative staff member."

Needless to say, more than idealism was needed to propel the Bank forward. McNamara's view of the Bank's development role was far broader than anyone would have guessed. No longer should the Bank satisfy itself with piecemeal projects. It needed a completely integrated approach to development that could assist clients in resolving the complex social and economic factors that hindered growth and contributed to poverty. After all, how could the Bank approve a loan for a new road in Kenya when the people living next to it would still be hungry and uneducated? Thus evolved a comprehensive reporting system where staff studied each borrower on a regular basis, requiring a massive increase in Economic and Development Policy Departments assigned to do the job. They molded this task in response to McNamara's passion for system and statistics. New and expanded visits were regularly scheduled to member countries, which were obliged to reserve officials' time for meetings and to expend scarce resources to provide for the Bank's ever increasing need for statistics.

Examining a sovereign economy as a whole, and adjusting individual project strategy from that wide viewpoint, required reorganization. In 1972, the Bank shifted from a structure of sector departments, such as power and transportation, where engineers were influential, to regional departments organized by country, where economists held sway. That year also brought the formal introduction of the Country Programming System (CPP), which remains in place today as the Country Assistance Strategy (CAS). To the first time reader, a CAS resembles the central plans produced by the old Soviet republics. The CAS reviews the subject economy—sector by sector—for dozens of single-spaced pages. The narratives employ supporting data tables and the back of the document contains a numbing amount of statistical charts.

Little hard analysis was found in these documents. Staffers learned that placing constructive critiques in a CAS was a career risk, because member government officials considered Bank differences with sovereign policies to be intrusive. The offending author generated internal problems if the client complained, a serious bureaucratic problem. The likelihood of such trouble is now remote. Committees write CASs with multiple redrafts to eliminate possible controversies. Many sections are "cut and paste" jobs from other CASs, where the language is proven not to offend. An "original" section might be drafted by one or two people, who submit it to colleagues for a critique. The authors then convene in meetings of 15 or 20 participants to review the chapter. Statements with a chance of causing difficulties end up watered down or eliminated.

As the Bank ground out CASs with increasing frequency in the 1970's, loan officers faced a competitive threat—the growth of the Euromarket. Stimulated by the need for money-center banks to recycle petrodollars, the Euromarket forgot poor country lending debacles of the 1920's and 1930's, and allowed Third World borrowers and commercial banks to meet on equal footing. Assured by prominent financiers, such as Citicorp's Walter Wriston, that countries do not go broke, the Euromarket grew from $70 billion in 1970 to $1.6 trillion in 1980. Four Latin American countries—Mexico, Brazil, Venezuela, and Argentina—and one Asian nation—Indonesia, became the Euromarket's top five borrowers. The advantages of going to the Euromarket for a loan instead of the Bank were many. Commercial banks processed transactions four or five times as fast as the Bank, and they didn't ask borrowers a lot of questions. Furthermore, commercial bank loans required few, if any, of the restrictive covenants or "conditionalities" that the Bank insisted upon. It is a testament to the staff's tenacity that loan volume increased so dramatically in the 70's, when at the same time commercial banks multiplied their Third World exposure many times over.

In part, the staff's job was made easier by McNamara's definition of "development lending," which included "social lending." The new emphasis increased the ability to pump out loans exponentially. Economic development now meant poverty alleviation. No longer were loan officers shackled to power plant and road loans. Development expanded into projects touching almost every aspect of human life—agricultural, housing construction, schools, health services, and population control—the list was endless. As the Bank and Eurodollar loans kept pouring in, some countries closed their economies to create a home-grown industrial base. High tariffs protected inefficient local firms, and host governments purchased and expropriated selective multinational businesses. New state-run industries, designed to reduce costly imports, received loan proceeds. In hindsight, the dubious quality of some projects boggles the imagination. Trinidad and Tobago, a Caribbean island nation of two million people, started its own automobile industry.

To avoid being labeled as the progenitor of industrial policy, the Bank refused loans to specific industries. Instead, it supported state-run development finance companies (DFC's), which then advanced the money to favored oligopolies and parastatals. A project's economic soundness or a borrower's credit worthiness was of secondary concern to the DFC's. No matter, support for DFC's approached 25 percent of total Bank lending by the late 1970's, in sharp contrast to the four percent share this sector received in the 1960's. A report by the Bank's evaluation office ("The Sustainability of DFC's in an Evolutionary Environment") recorded the dismal performance record. This report, like most others critical of the Bank's lending policies, was thrown onto the junk heap.

By the mid 1970's, McNamara's luster began to dull in the eyes of U.S. policymakers. Conservative congressmen were never entirely comfortable with McNamara's poverty alleviation policies, which they thought sounded like welfare schemes. Bank opposition to a U.S. initiative for a new development bank funded by oil-rich OPEC members did not help matters, and the institution damaged the relationship further by circulating plans to create a $30 billion subsidiary to compete with OPEC. The subsidiary intended to fund oil exploration in poor nations, as a means to lessen their dependence on the cartel's high priced oil. Things got testy after Jimmy Carter took office. Strongly dedicated to human rights, President Carter refused backing for loans to repressive Third World regimes. Maintaining that such loans were based solely on economic considerations, staffers thumbed their noses at Carter, and kept sending the offending projects to the Board. The United States, having 25 percent of the vote at the time, was outgunned. McNamara, meanwhile, went "native." Coopted by the bureaucracy, which was three-quarters non-American, he did little to support the Carter Administration's posture. A final humiliation occurred in 1979, when Vietnam invaded Cambodia and the Bank insisted on continuing its Vietnam loan program in the face of U.S. opposition.

The damage done to U.S.-Bank relations by these incidents was minimal when compared to the destruction rendered by Carter's attempts to reduce Bank salaries. As will be discussed later, Bank salaries and benefits are high by any standard. Nonetheless, Bank staffers, like employees in most organizations, pout about their compensation. They believe their lofty pay is a solemn right, like the lifetime tenure they enjoy. This feeling is stronger at the Bank than at comparable organizations because, as noted earlier, employees believe the Bank's mission is conducted on a moral plane far above those of mere governments or profit-making businesses. The resulting firestorm earned the U.S. the eternal enmity of Bank employees, despite the fact that the Carter administration acquiesced. Suspicion of American motives remains today as a strong undercurrent at the institution, which I liken to a dog biting its owner.

The Post McNamara Period

Although McNamara departed in 1981, his poverty alleviation thrust continued in the 1980's, a decade that saw the introduction of a new type of loan—a policy-based loan. Policy-based loans were not tied to a single project or sector. They provided money to recipients for balance of payments support or for subsidiary effects of economic policy change, such as the unemployment costs caused by cutting subsidies to local industries. Policy loans were sometimes called "structural adjustment loans" to denote the intent of the borrower to adjust its economic structure. This theme arose from a much delayed discovery: many projects failed because the borrower's economic system didn't allow a project to succeed. A good example is the Development Finance Corporation program mentioned earlier. In theory, DFC's boosted the private sector by allowing cheap funding. But, if a government permitted its economy to be dominated by oligopolies, no subsidized credit was likely to increase efficiencies until competition was installed. As Bank policy programs evolved, its loans started looking like IMF loans in one key respect: the borrower received a laundry list of reform requests as the price of obtaining a loan.

A. W. Clausen, McNamara's successor and the former chief executive officer of BankAmerica, pushed policy-based lending, yet the economic benefits to the borrower were even more difficult to measure than the return on a soft project like a hospital or a school. The Reagan administration objected to the lack of concrete outcomes in a number of these loans, vetoing in Board sessions financings directed to India, Philippines, Burma, and Guyana. It further objected to a proposed increase in the Bank's capital, correctly maintaining that the institution did not fulfill its catalytic role for the private sector. Mr. Clausen, unfortunately, surrendered to the bureaucracy as his predecessor did, and he backed the capital increase over the administration's protests.

In the 1980's, the Bank received a substantial amount of criticism for its failure to play a larger role in the international debt crisis. The problem began in 1982, when Mexico declared that it would not meet its financial obligations. Shortly thereafter, Brazil, another major Euromarket participant, defaulted and other developing nations followed suit. The Euroloan market quickly dried up and international banks faced huge losses. Resolving this crisis was tailor-made for a knowledgeable and reasonably neutral international financial organization, but the Bank was conflicted. It was owed over $100 billion by these same defaulting borrowers, and it traditionally received a priority claim over commercial bank obligations. Insiders knew that a Bank-arranged workout of private debt would involve the institution reducing the principal amount of its own loans, as the standard practice in bankruptcy is that all parties to a workout share the pain of a debtor's default. Taking a "haircut" on a loan, an action that is quite common for lenders to troubled borrowers, would have been deeply troubling to the Bank. It had always highlighted its special status to the buyers of its securities. Hadn't the Bank been fully paid on each loan? Management, it appeared, let the commercial banks work out the problem by themselves. Any portfolio write-down would have endangered the Bank's AAA bond rating.

Barber Conable, a leading Republican congressman, arrived as World Bank president in 1986. His 1987 reorganization was sabotaged by the bureaucracy, which used it as little more than an opportunity to reshuffle the deck chairs of existing management. The institution found his political skills useful and Mr. Conable was effective in convincing the U.S. Congress to approve a capital increase that allowed for higher loan volume. After that sizable task, he adopted a low profile. During his tenure, the International Finance Corporation, the Bank's private sector lending arm, expanded rapidly.

Conable's successor was Lewis Preston, the former head of J.P. Morgan, a prominent international bank. Appointed in 1992, he saw a major impetus by developing countries to depart from state run industry and to privatize their economies. These changes coincided with the fall of the Berlin Wall and the break-up of the Soviet Union. The Bank's support of these efforts widened, and it succeeded in recruiting the newly-independent Eastern European countries as members, many of which became fresh borrowers. The influx of the former Soviet states was a source of delight to staffers, who had tired of the frustration and failures associated with the existing client base. These socialist nations represented a clean slate upon which the Bank could test its latest development theories. The staff was optimistic, believing "maybe we can get it right this time."

More Problems Become Visible

In the middle of his Bank presidency, Mr. Preston's health deteriorated and he eased into a caretaker role. Toward the end of his term, Mexico, one of the developing world's largest debtors, underwent another financial crisis. Overnight, the peso devalued 50 percent, and the government faced default. A $53 billion bailout package orchestrated by the U.S. averted a Mexican bankruptcy and a possible domino default by other emerging market creditors.

Criticism of the institution expanded during the early 1990's, fed by lightning rod issues such as the Narmada project. Designed as a series of hydroelectric dams and irrigation projects in Central India, Narmada was an embarrassing white elephant. In pursuing this "trophy" project, the staff ignored its own resettlement policies, displacing 100,000 poor people without proper follow-up. The weakness in Bank environmental standards enhanced the malaria contraction rate in the reconstituted watershed, and, an independent commission concluded that the river system lacked sufficient water to support the irrigation schemes.

More important was the overall issue of project performance. Thirty six percent of Bank projects were classified as unsuccessful in 1992, up from 20 percent in 1986 and 10 percent in 1979. These statistics were derived from in-house evaluators rather than external auditors, who would have been tougher graders. Around the same time, an internal task force headed by Will Wapenhans, a former Bank executive, concluded that the staff failed to enforce loan conditionalities, which indicated that the Bank's "carrot and stick" approach to development lending was all carrot and no stick. Loan officers, according to the report, feared enforcing conditions annoyed borrowers. Unhappy borrowers meant less loan volume, which meant an unhappy management, which meant career problems. After a brief period in the spotlight, the Wapenhans report was shelved.

Finally, there was the issue of Bank staffing. The collapse of the centrally-planned economy took the bureaucracy totally unawares. Accustomed to doling out money to prop-up state-run industries, agriculture subsidies and protected oligopolies, the staff was unfamiliar with modern business practices; only a handful of the 8,000 permanent employees had any real private sector experience. Preston headed an institution that was unprepared, and unqualified, to provide economic advice to those poor nations seeking to promote a market based economy.

Jim Wolfensohn Takes Charge

1995—enter Jim Wolfensohn. A dynamic investment banker who lobbied heavily for the president's job, Wolfensohn was relatively young, and he promised to bring a new energy and focus to the institution, the problems of which were increasingly well known. A huge positive was the staff's optimism regarding his appointment. Frustrated by continuing poverty in the face of billions in development loans, morale had hit bottom, and even die-hard loyalists recognized that reform was necessary, as long as job security and staff compensation remained off limits. Another plus was that Wolfensohn, unlike the prior three presidents, was a progressive Democrat; and thus, his political leanings conformed to those of most of the staff. Although the employees' ideological commitment is best characterized as "limousine liberal," their shared sense of mission with Wolfensohn was an indicator of future cooperation.

His term began with a flurry of meetings, speeches, seminars, initiatives, and client visits, designed to motivate donors and recipients alike and to spark needed change and reform. The activities generated enthusiasm for a while, but within two years, it became apparent that Wolfensohn, like his immediate predecessor, was destined to be a caretaker, rather than a reformer.

Rather than limiting the scope of the Bank's work, which was spread too thin over too many countries and too many objectives, Wolfensohn intended to expand its reach, particularly into social and policy loans with their hard-to-measure results. Perhaps well intentioned, his initiatives usually turned out to be little more than publicity stunts, as crucial follow-up was missed time and time again. The lack of continuity resulted from both Wolfensohn's style and the staff's inertia. In his first time as the head of a large organization, Wolfensohn played the butterfly, flitting from subject to subject without dedicating major effort to core questions, such as "is the Bank's lending doing any good?" Even when he overcame his dilettante tendencies to focus on a specific proposal, he found things hard to implement for several reasons. First, he was "flying solo." Despite his ambitions, he failed to bring in outside managers that could push his mandates through the bureaucracy, without worrying about their next job in the development industry. Second, the Bank's authority lines run along the university model, whereby the World Bank president has limited power over the fiefdoms run by operating executives. Any institutional change required a collaborative effort requiring substantial face time with, and cajoling of, the affected parties. Wolfensohn did not apply the requisite internal effort, and he allocated his time too broadly. And finally, there was his management approach, which seemed mercurial, and relied, occasionally, on intimidating subordinates. This technique can be effective on Wall Street, but it was inappropriate at the buttoned-down Bank, where criticism is offered indirectly. The word got around, and his persuasive ability within the institution diminished as a result.

As he passed into his second term, Wolfensohn's desire to institute meaningful reforms waned, and he seemed content to play the globetrotting ambassador, handing out grants to poor countries and posing for photo-ops with schoolchildren. Rather than fight the bureaucratic mandarins for improvements, he resigned himself to "go along" status and parroted the party line that only more loans alleviated poverty. Along the way, he selected a few pet causes that antagonized no one, such as debt relief for the poorest countries, extra funding for AIDS prevention and anti-corruption incentives for enlightened governments. He also deflected damning criticism from several outside studies on the Bank and successfully placed more staff in field offices.

His tenure saw a number of notable financial events in the developing world. In 1997, several emerging Asian nations—Thailand, Malaysia, Indonesia, and South Korea—suffered massive currency devaluation and the specter of sovereign bankruptcy. Huge bailouts, engineered by the U.S. Treasury and the IMF, prevented defaults and limited the magnitude of subsequent recessions. In 1998, Russia reneged on its debts, costing investors billions, and three years later, Argentina, one of the Bank's biggest borrowers and one of the largest emerging market creditors, went bankrupt. These setbacks represented temporary obstacles to the integration of large developing countries into Western portfolios. By the time of Wolfensohn's departure in 2005, all had been forgotten and emerging market investment was booming, with capital flows hitting new highs.

Paul Wolfowitz Becomes President

In March 2005, Paul Wolfowitz received the nomination to head the Bank. On the surface, he was as qualified as his predecessors. Although lacking financial expertise, his foreign relations and international development credentials were impeccable, and he had the ear of George W. Bush, president of the largest shareholder. The latter fact was a sore point, because, as noted, the staff is heavily pro-Democrat in its political leanings, and thinks the Republican Party is out to get them. At the same time, he arrived with considerable baggage, attributable to his pivotal role in pushing the unpopular Iraq war while serving as deputy secretary of defense. In responding to critics, he made the proper conciliatory statements to appease the opposition, and he reassured staff that there was nothing to worry about. On his first day, he paid tribute to Wolfensohn's ten year reign and added that no organizational makeover was necessary within the Bank to ensure its effectiveness in meeting priorities. In an institution that cries out for change, Mr. Wolfowitz was quickly neutered. By acquiescing, the Bush administration damaged hopes of reform.

In his first 20 months, Wolfowitz kept a low profile, and his few initiatives focused on established Wolfensohn themes such as protecting the environment, fighting corruption, and curtailing AIDS. His one challenge was facing up to Idriss Derby, the authoritarian leader of Chad, a desperately impoverished country located in Saharan Africa. Several years earlier, the Bank assisted Exxon and Chevron, two major oil companies, in financing a \$4.2 billion, 640-mile pipeline that delivers oil from Chad's southwestern oil fields to Cameroon's Atlantic Coast. Although the Bank's portion totaled just four percent of the cost, the oil giants considered its participation as inexpensive insurance, given the risks of doing business in Chad. In return for facilitating the deal, the Bank got President Derby to place the new-found oil revenues into a London escrow account, whereby the money could be properly accounted for, and then devoted to poverty reduction. The innovative idea intended to reverse the trend of other resource-wealthy Third World countries, where large portions of export revenues are siphoned off into corrupt officials' secret accounts, grandiose construction projects and unnecessary military expenditures. The resolution of the problem was "of great interest to other countries facing the challenge of transforming their oil wealth into benefits for their people, to donors attempting to solve the problem of the resource curse, and to energy-hungry industrialized countries searching for new and stable sources of oil," according to Ian Gary and Nikki Reisch, authors of "Chad Oil Miracle or Mirage?"

When the petrodollars began flowing, Chadian officials received new Mercedes and the military obtained fresh cash. By late 2005, the government broke its promise to devote oil dollars to poverty, and Wolfowitz sprang into action, cutting off further loans and freezing the escrow account. In the negotiations that followed, he blinked first, doubling the oil money provided to the government without oversight, bringing it to 25 percent of the total. By not sticking to its guns, the Bank set itself up for another crisis in a few years, when Derby will inevitably ask for 50 percent in unrestricted funds; and thus, the Bank jeopardized its future ability to implement similar projects.

V.
DEVELOPMENT LOANS AND THEIR ISSUES

Why do wealthy countries provide assistance to poor nations in the first place? Foreign aid, as generally defined, is a government-to-government mechanism, though the citizens of certain wealthy countries have long histories of charitable giving to international causes. To start, the donor government has to decide what portion of its budget to set aside for aid and, given the nature of international relations, it is naïve to presume such aid is given entirely for humanitarian reasons. Political ties play a role as well as the donor's geo-strategic concerns. For example, a large part of U.S. foreign aid is directed to Israel and Egypt, important U.S. allies in an oil-rich region. Commercial interests between nations also influence aid flows. Japan, to illustrate, has a keen interest in Southeast Asia to facilitate trade flows. It directs a substantial portion of its aid budget to Asian countries.

Grants versus Loans

The preponderance of foreign aid comes in two forms: grants and loans. Grants have no repayment obligations and are essentially gifts with strings attached. For example, a recent U.S. $75 million grant to Senegal required specific health initiatives in rural areas. Loans require the recipient to pay interest and principal on a pre-set schedule, and they are typically denominated in the donor's home currency or in a widely-used international currency. Like grants, the loans are restricted in their objectives and uses, focusing on specific sectors such as transportation, health, or education. Because of the repayment obligation, a loan puts less stress on the donor's budget than a grant, and there is a sense that a recipient country "buys into" a project when repayment is involved.

To be considered foreign aid, a loan should be "concessional" or "lender of last resort." Together, these adjectives describe loans that are unobtainable in the commercial marketplace. The interest rate is lower, the maturity is longer, or both conditions exist. In certain cases, the poor country cannot obtain credit on any basis, and the loan is a lender-of-last-resort obligation.

For example, the best US$ loan terms Ukraine can expect in the international market are a 7.5 percent interest rate and a 10 year maturity. At the World Bank, it borrows at 5.5 percent for 20 years.

United States Makes Many Development Loans

Many nations use development loans to further domestic polices. By way of illustration, the U.S. federal government is a huge provider of development finance, covering many sectors of economic and social activity. One of its largest loan programs promotes college education. Students, by virtue of their age, do not have solid credit histories, so the government is a lender of last resort, guaranteeing over $50 billion of concessional loans annually to support higher education. Advanced schooling supports democracy and economic progress, but the program has financial underpinnings as well, since college graduates earn more than non-degreed workers, and should have the future wherewithal to repay the loans.

World Bank financing often fails the basic standards placed on U.S. student loans. As noted previously, the majority of loans go to countries that already have access to commercial credit. Of course, capital markets have been kind to emerging markets over the last five years and this situation can change if a prominent recipient experiences a meltdown. But, for now, the institution does not function as a lender of last resort and many loans accrue to nations that can borrow elsewhere. In that Bank loans carry lower interest rates and longer maturities than market-based instruments, they are concessionary. Unlike student loans, however, the connection between a Bank project and a future borrower income is extremely tenuous and the institution's economists have never refuted this assertion.

The Beginning of a Development Loan

On a regular basis, senior management assigns multi-year budgets to each regional department head, who then allocates loan volumes among relevant countries according to several criteria: the political strength of the potential recipients at headquarters, the amount of money they already owe the Bank, the frequency of Bank operations in the country, and the ability of the Bank to engage in a ground-breaking, newsworthy operation. Once a country's loan allocation is set, the regional head and country manager find ways to spend it.

The Europe and Central Asia Region includes Albania, an impoverished nation of three million people nestled between Greece and Serbia. Albania's loan budget for 2007 was $50 million. The first step for task managers (or loan officers) contemplating new projects is to consult the Bank's research on Albania. Every few years, the Bank prepares extensive economic reports on its clients, which are complemented on an ongoing basis by technical studies and academic papers covering specific problem areas. Although this material has a "cut and paste" quality that makes Bank reports seem generic, it presents numerous public and private sectors that can use outside capital and expertise.

Specific projects within sectors are suggested and estimated price tags are attached. (One report on Guyana, a tiny South American nation, showed projects costing $900 million over a three-year period, an amount more than half the country's annual GNP). In Albania, proposed projects run the gamut, from new highways to disease control to agricultural support, but no numerical ranking is determinable for two principal reasons. One, Bank evaluations lack cost-benefit analysis because most program benefits are either opaque or unquantifiable. And two, borrowing governments disapprove of economists assigning priorities, even when the Bank is the ultimate provider of the funds, because such rankings somehow infringe on the borrower's "sovereignty." Armed with a list of 20 to 25 projects, Bank managers consult with government leaders on which investments are acceptable. As with any public spending discussion, the talks become politicized and developmental rigor is overlooked. In making proposals, the staff might hope to introduce a concept that is new to the borrower, such as helping the environment, in order to impress their superiors with the modicum of differentiation that passes for creativity at the Bank. The finance minister, in contrast, might seek projects that provide jobs and foreign exchange. Once the borrower and the Bank narrow the list to three or four items, the projects are refined by a team of staffers and outside consultants, who literally invade the country for weeks on end, compiling information and statistics for their appraisal reports.

Cost Benefit Analysis

Cost benefit analysis for projects is best described as an "accounting framework" for making decisions. It calculates the monetary value of a project's benefits over a future time period. Against these benefits are deducted the corresponding costs, and the net difference for each year is discounted to the present. The discount rate reflects the time value of money, as well as the perceived level of project risk, so near-term benefits are assigned higher weightings than far-off benefits. The beauty of cost benefit analysis is that it provides a single yardstick—the net present value—that can be compared and contrasted among different project types.

In the case of a student loan, for example, the initial four years represent costs, reflecting tuition, board, and forfeited income, and then follows 10 years of debt repayment. Offsetting these costs are the 40 years of extra income, realized by the borrower having a college degree rather than a high school diploma. See Exhibit 5.1.

Obviously, Exhibit 5.1 excludes the non-financial benefits of a college education, such as intellectual enlightenment and self-awareness, but it enables the borrower and lender to reduce the subjectivity of the investment decision. A high net present value suggests a good investment and a low level indicates a bad one.

Exhibit 5.1 College Loan Cost-Benefit Analysis
($000)

	1	2	3	4	5	6	7	8	9	10	Beyond 10 Years
Benefits	$---	$---	$---	$---	$10	$12	$15	$18	$20	$23	$ 900
					Extra Income			*Debt Repayment*			
Costs	30	30	30	30	6	6	6	6	6	6	24
		College Expense									
Net Benefits	$(30)	$(30)	$(30)	$(30)	$ 4	$ 6	$ 9	$12	$14	$17	$ 876

Present Value of Net Benefits at a 12% Discount Rate = $15,000.

Optimally, a development institution like the Bank, which has limited resources, should use the cost-benefit approach to rank projects scientifically. Those with the highest net present value merit acceptance, as illustrated in Exhibit 5.2.

Exhibit 5.2 Hypothetical Selection of Development Projects

	Project Type	Net Present Value
Accepted	Road maintenance	$50 million
	Power generation	30
	Privatization assistance	20
Rejected	Financial modernization	10
	Irrigation dam	5
	Structural adjustment	(8)

The practical difficulties of estimating benefits and costs cannot be underestimated, and the methodology, by its nature, involves many value judgments. It is not foolproof, but it provides a systematic aspect to loan decisions. Robert Hahn, head of the AEI-Brookings Institute on Regulatory Policy, called cost benefit analysis a "bulwark against moralism and special interests;" and the Bank would do well to emphasize it in lieu of an ad hoc procedure.

The Pipeline

With little regard for cost-benefit analysis, the laundry list of project concepts is "firmed up" into discrete assignments requiring further research. Separate teams of Bank professionals and consultants study the proposals, perhaps over six to twelve months, and discard those that do not meet the Bank's or Albania's investment criteria. For the projects that survive the screening process, there is a place in the pipeline, and another 12 to 18 months of preparation and documentation.

The frequency of certain project categories in Albania and the rest of Eastern Europe are an important factor in the Department's allocations. For political reasons in (and out of) the institution, the staff does not want to make loans in the same category repeatedly. "Cookie cutter" transactions may be appropriate in many instances, but they give third parties the impression that the World Bank's job is easy, so Regional Departments make a concerted effort to diversify themes. Road projects are followed by adjustment loans that are followed by social financings. In fact, if one loan officer mentions to another that he is working on a highway loan, the sarcastic response is, "What, another road project?" The helter skelter nature of choices opens the Bank to a charge of dilettantism, which is supported by Albania's fractured 2000 to 2006 approval list. See Exhibit 5.3.

Exhibit 5.3	Albania Project Loans 2000-2006	
Project Name	Approval Year	Amount (US$ Millions)
Business Environment Reform	2006	9
Avian Influenza Control	2006	5
Education Excellence	2006	15
Health System Modernization	2006	15
South East Europe Energy	2005	27
Coastal Zone Management	2005	18
Natural Resources Development	2005	12
Poverty Reduction Support	2004	10
Water Resources Management	2004	15
Water & Ecosystems Management	2004	5
Power Sector Generation	2004	25
Poverty Reduction	2003	18
Road Maintenance	2003	13
Community Works	2003	15
Municipal Wastewater	2003	15
Road Maintenance	2002	17
Financial Sector Adjustment	2002	15
Poverty Reduction	2002	20
Power Sector Rehabilitation	2002	30
Pilot Fishery Development	2002	6
Agricultural Services	2001	10
Social Services	2001	10
Trade & Transport	2000	8
Financial Sector Assistance	2000	7
Education Reform	2000	12
Legal & Judicial Reform	2000	9
Public Administration Reform	2000	9
Water Supply Rehabilitation	2000	10

The 28 loans in Exhibit 5.3 touched a dozen different themes, and it is debatable whether any of the small projects had a lasting impact. Indeed, a better use of resources might have been for the Bank to target one or two key problem areas. Given the country's tiny size, a tight focus could have made a significant contribution. For example, proper electricity supply is a *sina qua non* of economic development, yet Albania has suffered severe shortages for the last ten years. The 2006 winter was especially problematic, with the capital, Tirana, subject to daily blackouts lasting as long as 18 hours. Since 1995, the Bank authorized six energy projects with a total commitment of $127 million, and in 2005 it claimed to have "taken the lead role in this sector." But its piecemeal approach in Albania and inability to push energy reforms paints the Bank as a helpless giant.

Exhibit 5.4   Twelve Themes Covered By
28 Albanian Projects, 2000-2006

1. Agriculture and Irrigation
2. Community
3. Education
4. Energy
5. Environment
6. Health
7. Legal, Judicial and Public Administrative Reform
8. Pilot Fishery
9. Poverty Reduction
10. Road Maintenance
11. Social Services
12. Water Distribution

Loan Conditions Promote Development

As the World Bank and the borrower settle in on a proposed project, there begins a series of negotiations on what conditions accompany the loan. A new power plant may alleviate electricity outages in the short-run, but if the national utility sells energy at a fraction of the production cost (as it does in Albania), the project is not developmental. Albanians use electricity in a wasteful manner, such as home heating, when conservation or alternative energies, such as natural gas, are appropriate. In the past, the Bank requested conditions to promote efficient electricity use, such as a gradual shift to cost-based pricing, and to encourage effective generation, such as a utility privatization. The government seemed to agree in principle, but the proposed conditions met stiff resistance as political leaders feared a constituent backlash from higher prices. In 2007, electricity rates are still below cost and the utility is still a government-run monopoly.

Because loan conditions appear to impose painful adjustments to "business as usual," they are the biggest source of complaints from a borrower's political and business elite, who say the Bank takes unfair advantage. No matter, time has shown that the loan officers concede to borrower requests for weaker conditions and fail to enforce the modest terms they do require. A review of Albanian loan conditions suggests the Bank's requirements are far from onerous. An agricultural loan asks that a satisfactory Plant Variety Protection law be submitted to Parliament, but the law doesn't have to be enacted or enforced. A health modernization loan mandates that Albania adopt a framework that facilitates the establishment of a primary health care framework and the enrollment of beneficiaries with health care providers. However, adopting a framework is a far cry from ensuring the system is set up and actually enrolls patients. Even if the system activates, the loan has no guarantee that quality health care is delivered. A 2006 reform project aims to encourage unregistered businesses to transition into the formal sector, where they can better access finance and trade, and thus strengthen the local export base. Regardless, the only concrete covenant was for the borrower to (a) submit a plan to update trade inspection facilities by 2007, and (b) to implement it thereafter. In sum, the loan conditions can hardly be called coercive, and they barely touched on the country's pervasive corruption, a major obstacle. One can make the argument that development and Albania's populace would be better served if the World Bank held the government's feet to the fire.

Defining Project Success

As with loan conditions, the definition of project success is a product of negotiation between the Bank and the borrower. Success is much easier to characterize in meeting physical objectives (e.g., completing a road or a power plant) than in fulfilling social programs or achieving policy reforms. For the minority of projects that have economic-rate-of-returns, the projected ERR is compared to the actual ERR. It is to the advantage of both the staff and the borrower that success be couched in opaque terms, rather than objective measurements. In this way, after project completion, both sides declare victory. In Albania (and other recipients), this situation plays out in two ways. One, positive outcomes are broadly worded, enabling the Bank's graders (i.e., itself) plenty of wiggle room. For example, the Coastal Zone Clean-Up Project indicated goals as "enhancing the capacity of authorities to manage coastal resources, strengthening coastal water minority network and assisting communities in protecting resources" and so on. "Enhancing, strengthening and assisting" can be interpreted in any number of ways. Two, the staff assigns to each project dozens of little objectives. If the Bank and government fails on one, the poor grade is overshadowed by passing marks on others. To its credit, the institution's internal assessor critiqued these tactics in a 2005 Albania report, recommending that staff "establish monitorable and realistic targets for outcomes and design interventions (aid) to meet these targets."

Implementation and Monitoring

The Bank is the principal designer and financier of its projects, but it receives input from a variety of sources. Recipient governments, other multilateral or bilateral aid donors, local and international non-profit groups, supposed beneficiaries, and global aid agencies are among those that weigh in on proposed projects. The actual implementation of the project—i.e., providing the requisite goods, services, or policy changes—is the recipient's responsibility. Because Third World governments frequently lack the technical skills and administrative resources to fulfill projects, the staff may recommend in-house training or outside consultants to assist in the implementation process. Indeed, the provision of such services is now a cottage industry in the development business, employing thousands of Westerners who work on projects funded by the Bank and its imitators.

The challenge of getting a project to work is typically underestimated by staffers. On the one hand is the difficulty of getting anything done in an emerging market environment. In my experience, a good rule of thumb is a task that takes three months in the U.S. requires six months in Latin America, nine months in Asia and 18 months in Africa. Even Third World projects supervised by Western governments, rather than multilateral aid organizations, run into problems. Consider the following *New York Times* synopsis of a joint report by the Pentagon and U.S. State Department:

Five years after the fall of the Taliban, the American-trained police force in Afghanistan is largely incapable of carrying out routine law enforcement work, and the managers of the $1.1 billion training program cannot say how many officers are actually on duty or where thousands of trucks and other equipment issued to police units have gone.

On the other hand is the inherent problem of operating through a poor country government. Civil servants may lack urgency, be overworked, or be susceptible to bribes. The attendant risk of failure is high, and I compare the obstacles to success as equivalent to those encountered in a venture capital start-up, where seven out of ten do not survive.

The government issue is paramount, according to George Ayittey, a member of the Task Force on Multilateral Banks (1998), sponsored by the Center for Strategic and International Studies. In the report, he states the following:

> Government as it is known in the United States does not exist in many parts of Africa. What exists in Africa is a 'Mafia' or 'Vampire State'—that is, a state hijacked by a coterie of con artists, gangsters, and crooks to enrich themselves. The richest persons in Africa are heads of state and ministers. Government is not a vehicle to serve but to fleece the people, through confiscatory taxes, levies, and other state controls.

By way of reference, Albania's corruption perception index ranked below most African nations, according to Transparency International.

Once a project is funded and money is released to the recipient, the loan officer thinks his job is finished. But ongoing monitoring is a necessity, not only to help the borrower achieve results, but also to prevent aid from being diverted through shenanigans. With its emphasis on loan volume, monitoring is not high on the Bank's priority list, and it can be a difficult task, particularly when objectives are so vaguely articulated. Pronouncements by its public relations machine in recent years suggest more attention is being paid to this area, as well as to corruption, where Wolfensohn and Wolfowitz have promised action. In reality, however, the Bank's forensic audit ability over aid flows is limited, and it impacts government corruption at the tiniest of margins, given the widespread nature of the problem.

Evaluation After Project Completion

A commercial bank making a loan to a low-income country considers success as full repayment. But the World Bank, as a development institution, holds itself to a higher standard. Success encompasses both the repayment of the loan and the attainment of the social, policy, or physical objectives embodied in the related project.

For the Bank, repayment is not a problem. It is a preferred creditor even when its recipient countries default on commercial debt, and Bank management has the flexibility to paper over bad loans with new loans, thus assuring continued debt service. In recent years, outside pressure forced the Bank to acknowledge that this tactic was burdensome to some clients, and in 2006, the institution wrote off $33 billion in loans to its poorest borrowers, offering numerous countries breathing room in their finances.

The delivery of developmental goals normally requires several years. The construction of a power plant, the modernization of a school system or the improvement of a public administration, for example, are lengthy tasks, and they are usually accompanied by policy advice that must run through the borrower's legislative and bureaucratic process. After money has been spent and the project's product, service, or advice has been "delivered," the Bank's staff evaluates the loan's effectiveness from a development point of view. This comprehensive analysis tends to take place five to seven years after the loan's initial disbursement, and perhaps two to three years after the project is finished. Because of internal job shifts over the intervening period, the team evaluating the project is different from the group that appraised, processed, and closed the loan. This "fresh look" brings surprising candor in many instances, and provides the basis for one of six project ratings, ranging from highly unsatisfactory to highly satisfactory.

For one-quarter of the projects, the internal audit division completes its own evaluation, assigning a team of staffers and consultants to review implementation results and developmental impacts. The reports are quite lengthy and involve statistical analyses, surveys and in-country interviews. For those projects with an economic-rate-of-return, there may be a recalculation of the number, reflecting post-completion costs and benefits.

Although the institution places its failure rate at 25 percent, it has never allowed an outside verification of this statistic, and it is reasonable to presume that an independent third party might arrive at a higher number. Examples of unsuccessful projects include the following:

- When a road is constructed and not enough people use the road for it to be an economical investment;
- When a new power plant suffers huge cost overruns, making the electricity too expensive;
- When an education loan finances new schools, but no new teachers or books;
- When an environmental project creates resentment because the local community still lacks access to basic services;
- When a poverty reduction loan is a temporary jobs program, rather than development project with lasting potential;
- When a loan to strengthen civil service institutions is overwhelmed by new political leadership that is lukewarm to reforms;
- When public housing is built for the poor, only to have the government rent it to the well-off;
- When portions of loan proceeds are stolen by corrupt officials; and
- When a policy loan is made to a nation that has no intention of adjusting its policies.

In those reports that get a failing grade, the culprits are depressingly similar and frequently include the following:

- Inability of the recipient government to implement the project properly ("institutional weakness" in Bank jargon);
- Overly ambitious goals on the part of Bank staff;
- Unrealistic view on project risks by staff;
- Inadequate attention to project design and monitoring, particularly for projects that are experimental; and
- Naïve view on the length of time needed for policy reform in developing country, particularly when there is little recipient "buy in."

Given the Bank's long tenure, a systematic avoidance of these factors should be the rule, but history repeats itself. One critic, Bruce Rich of the Environmental Defense Fund, calls the institution "the Don't Remember Bank." At one in-house seminar, two participants concluded the following:

> My own observation from working with many different types of Bank projects is that we have not evaluated risks very well. Recently, we looked at our investments in the power sector, and we discovered we had made the same mistakes too many times to write them off as random events.
>
> Because World Bank loans are guaranteed by governments, it is reasonably natural for Bank staff to consider unimportant the risks behind Bank-supported projects.

Of course, the loan officers could reduce risks if they read the Bank's own audit reports and research studies, but much of this information appears "stove piped" among internal departments, so lessons learned are not always incorporated in new projects. As one consultant said, "Bank operations often contradict the research department's advice." And the staffers might pay more attention to potential problems if bad investments carried career disincentives, but that is not the case. One executive indicated; "I am not aware of any staff member ever being censured for producing bad estimates on a project or for having forecasts that went wrong."

In deemphasizing results, the staff takes its cue from top management. As noted earlier, in 2006, the budget for public relations and publications approximated $80 million, or four times the $20 million budget for project evaluations. This disparity suggests that the Bank's economic development claims are put forward for propagandistic and not for scientific reasons. The employees interpret this message and act accordingly.

VI.
THE STAFF

B y any account, the World Bank's staff is one of the most educated in the world. Almost 8,500 strong, excluding the IFC, which I cover later, the staff includes over 4,000 professional employees. Hundreds of these "higher level" staffers have doctoral degrees and many are graduates of prestigious universities. They are a dedicated bunch, working long hours and traveling thousands of miles away from home in their jobs. That these efforts routinely result in costly failures is a tragedy. Yet the mishaps are the result of the staff selling out its intellectual principles as much as they are the product of an outmoded organization.

One only has to read a sampling of loan reports to conclude that the higher level staff, far from being an objective group of development professionals, acts as a shill for generating new loans. Under constant pressure to originate projects that generate more loans, the staff churns out reports chock full of questionable assertions and useless statistics, and lacking the kind of academic proofs that many provided in their own dissertations.

Particularly disturbing is the staff's disregard for the scientific method, the rigorous procedure that includes the study of hypothesis, induction, theory, and method of explanation. Economic development is not a "hard" science, such as physics, where experiments are repeatable, but it has advanced to the point where a sufficient number of causative patterns have been observed, giving practitioners a greater degree of confidence in making conclusions than their counterparts in softer sciences such as sociology. Despite this framework, the staff has an annoying tendency to ignore local factors in favor of universal truths. Loan reports feature absolute statements such as, "The stagnation in the growth of tourism in Gambia has been caused by a lack of infrastructure" or "Decreased trade in Benin resulted from the deterioration of coastal shipping facilities." Rarely are these causal relationships supported by scholarly research, which means the collection of data through observation and measurement and the formulation of tests and hypotheses. For example, tourism revenues in Gambia may have dropped because of the recession in France, an important tourist source, or a general fear of airline terrorism; the decrease in Benin trade activity may have reflected an economic decline in the economy or the financial collapse of an important manufacturer. But, the systematic pursuit of causes is rarely in evidence, and the proposed solutions come easily, since they are almost identical for similar problems. The unique political and social factors of individual countries that contribute to poverty, and hamper the solution, receive short shrift.

The reductionist style of analysis is perfect for a staff that is largely cloistered in the diplomatic confines of Washington, DC and that restricts itself, even when traveling, to meeting fellow scholars and bureaucrats. However, the pure, stable, and controlled processes set forth in an economics textbook are no substitute for a concentrated study of a real developing economy. Too many times the staff's conclusions are centered in a dangerous ignorance of the facts. Theories conceived by the project teams are verified through contacts with other theoreticians, as Bankers rarely talk to the supposed beneficiaries of the World Bank's largesse—be they landless peasants on the one hand or active businessmen on the other. A Washington lawyer who had worked on European privatizations remembers the institution's intransigence on confronting realities in the field, "The (World) Bankers would say: 'The policy is this. We don't care if it doesn't work. This is our policy.'" Reports concentrate on the positive side of the project's characteristics, such as the forecast benefits, and pay little attention to the negatives, such as the risk of failure and the borrower's added debt burden. The June 2006 loan to Haiti's state utility, for example, stressed the government's intentions to collect long overdue electric bills and to stop illegal hook-ups, despite its inability to do so for the prior five loans.

Once a proposal gains momentum, internal meetings regarding its validation become irrelevant. By that time, the project and its loan appear on internal budgets and the top brass counts on it to fill the annual loan quota. Nevertheless, as a project advances through the various steps of approval, the team gets together regularly. The meetings have an academic flavor because the loan officer defends his project before his peers—but without the intellectual exactitude of the university setting. Once the report reaches the intermediate stage, the attendees take Board approval as a given; and consequently, the questions nibble around the project's edges rather than challenge its fundamentals, such as whether the loan is developmental or if the country can repay. This fact notwithstanding, the meetings endure for hours as fellow colleagues delight in scoring meaningless pedantic points and demonstrating their knowledge of arcane theories. A typical outcome is that the loan officer rewrites the report and gathers more data.

The minutia that is required in some of these preliminary reports is absurd. In one meeting on a $120 million Jamaican electrical plant that I was a part of, three Bankers argued for more than an hour in front of fifteen colleagues, on (i) whether the energy consumption statistics in the report should include firewood, which poor Jamaicans obtain by chopping down trees in the countryside; and (ii) whether the Bank should impose a conditionality on the Jamaican government, stipulating that citizens should pay an "energy equivalence" tax on the firewood they cut secretly in the middle of the night. The theoretical purity of the project depended on all kinds of energy being priced efficiently, according to my Banker colleagues, who conveniently ignored the government monopoly on gasoline retailing. Grudgingly, the group decided to forgo charging the poor for firewood. As a practical matter, it was crazy to have the government patrolling the forests at night anyway.

Need for Information

All of the World Bank's borrowers are repeat customers and learn to tolerate the institution's obsession with trivial information. The recipients are also accustomed to the long trips that the staffers use to refine their reports. In fact, it is not unusual for a loan officer to spend five consecutive weeks in a country, visiting government ministries of one sort or another, if he is not based "in country" already. The time spent is in the midst of comfortable surroundings, such as the capital city's finest hotels, which always have special rates for Bank personnel. The trips are called "missions" in Bank jargon. Thus, when an outsider calls a traveling staffer, the assistant inevitably answers that "so and so is on mission." *Funk & Wagnalls Dictionary* defines the word "mission" as "any body of persons sent some place in order to perform or accomplish a specific work or service." Bank missions include ten or more individuals who collectively monopolize large blocks of government time. In Peru, for example, missions take up entire floors of Lima's best hotels for weeks, and missions from different departments fall over each other in the same hotels.

Accompanying the staff group on a mission are several consultants. The term "consultant" in most organizations means an individual working on a temporary assignment, but Bank consultants are frequently full-time employees, prohibited from taking duties with other corporations. In fact, in 2006 over 1,500 consultants and temporary employees worked on a full-time basis, costing an estimated $180 million. Returning from a trip to South America, I met one of my former colleagues returning from a five-week mission to Brazil. His group consisted of himself and seven consultants! Originally filling in for short-term personnel gaps, the consultants are a permanent fixture, but they endure a second class status. Unlike their employee brethren, the consultants have little job security and serve at the whim of the loan officers, who have Rolodexes full of people willing to work in this capacity. Many full-time consultants have no express technical specialty, and, not surprisingly, they are frequently assigned tedious tasks that the loan officer has neither the time nor the inclination to complete. Others are Bank retirees, who need a little extra cash; they are especially valuable since they know the process.

Over a series of trips, the employee and consultant team puts together a loan report for the Board of Directors. Inevitably, the borrower's image and the project's benefits are inflated, thus making it easier to palm the loan off to its Board, which, in any case, plays the same asset building game as the staff. If there is a doubt on the Board, the staff is forewarned, and the borrower's finance minister might be asked to lobby the recalcitrant director. A good example of this last minute politicking was the Jamaican Energy Project. The U.S. and Canadian executive directors had misgivings about the project, thinking it could have been financed through the private sector. A few days before the Board meeting, both the Jamaican finance minister and the energy minister visited the directors in Washington to plead the government's case. This occurred at the same time that Jamaica recorded its fifth year of refusing to service its commercial bank debt. Needless to say, the energy loan was approved by unanimous vote.

Job Hopping

The borrowers suffer from the incessant job hopping within the organization. Some years ago, employees were rightly encouraged to broaden their skills by changing jobs every so often. One might change territory, for example. After covering Africa for a number of years, a staff member might work with Asia. Or, an agricultural loan officer might shift to health loans. Now, this goal of broadening skills is interpreted to mean that an employee's chances of promotion are lessened unless he changes jobs regularly. As a result, staff members constantly look to switch departments every few years, and the departments then lack the in-country expertise needed to provide optimal service. Besides placing people without country-specific knowledge in a geographical area, the system discourages the monitoring of projects by those employees who know the project best, i.e, those who supervised the loan's initiation. All too frequently, a loan officer, fresh from completing his "deal," moves to greener pastures, leaving behind mistakes to be faced by the poor borrower and the new transferee.

The Staff's Dilemma

The staff's emphasis in ensuring that they as individuals receive full credit for making a loan lies in the institution's poor productivity. In the fiscal year ending June 30, 2006, for example, the full-time staff of 10,000 employees and consultants generated 279 new loans, or one loan for every 36 positions. See Exhibit 6.1. Excluding non-loan-originating staff drops this number to 25. The relative dearth of transactions entails anxiety for the professionals, because the annual credit for loans, expressed in the form of favorable personnel reviews, promotions, and raises, is spread over just a fraction of the staff. The pressure to eliminate shared credit is thus intense, because an employee plays an important project role only every few years. The temptation to process faulty loans and to ignore follow-up work is thus hard to resist. No one in charge has made an honest attempt to resolve the staff's dilemma, and there is scant evidence member nations even care.

Exhibit 6.1 World Bank Loan Summary
(In US$ Billions, except Number of New Loans)

	2004	2005	2006
Loan Disbursements	17	19	21
Principal Repayment	20	16	15
New Outflow	(3)	3	6
Loans Outstanding	226	225	230
Number of New Loans	245	278	279

The amount of deadwood maintained in the professional ranks is another source of frustration for responsible employees. In my experience, about one-third of the staff does two-thirds of the work; one-third carries their own weight; and one-third is totally unproductive. In fact, the latter group infringes on the efforts of the first two, by talking on in meetings, delaying reports through incompetence, and interrupting others with endless chitchat. Because the civil service set-up prohibits outright firings, the personnel supervisors attempt to reassign lazy employees to non-essential jobs. Considered internally as a fruitless effort, the African Department is a favorite dumping ground.

It does not take a $100 million loan to attract employee interest. Even small financings are sought by staffers who realize they have few chances to shine. Records from 2006 provide a good illustration. In that year, loan approvals included smaller projects such as a $30 million loan to Ecuador for social services, a $12 million loan to Belize for a power station, a $26 million loan to Burkina Faso for family planning services, and a $14 million loan to Uganda for cotton production. Top management likes smaller projects added to the portfolio, which is heavily represented by large loans to the top seven borrowers—India, Brazil, China, Mexico, Bangladesh, Indonesia, and Turkey, which, as noted earlier, comprise 40 percent of the loan portfolio. Smaller recipients, like Barbados, Costa Rica, and Sri Lanka, complain about the large nations receiving too high a proportion of the funds. The small projects reduce the irritation.

In both large and small loan reports, the analysis of poor country problems is depressingly similar, as are the proposed solutions. It seems as if every borrower is asked by the staff to reduce government deficits, improve management, raise taxes, eliminate tariffs and sell off state-run businesses—all at the same time! Luckily, the borrowers realize that the Bank's policy advice has little or no enforcement action behind it. Since the 1990's, repeated studies have shown that the Bank values intentions more than results.

Many recipients have terrible records in managing Bank—financed projects. This fact rarely enters project reports. The staff does immeasurable harm to its clients by avoiding critical examination of new loans, especially since many of the related projects are little more than a roll of the dice. Based on prior experiences and internal studies, the staff knows that most borrowers have neither the management talent, technical skills, nor physical infrastructure to deliver the services contemplated by projects, but the institution never tires of pushing more debt on these beleaguered nations.

Risks are down-played in appraisal reports full of language designed to dull the senses and confuse the intellect. Meaningless jargon is jammed into reports that repeat generalities such as "The program aims to reorient the economy toward competitive markets and improving incentives for private sector participation," or "Delays in implementation could result from weak institutional implementation capacity and changing political priorities." In the end, the Bank's constituents are discouraged from reading the documents. Those who read and understand the material often discover that the reports' analyses are wrong. But these findings hardly perturb top management. As indicated earlier, one-quarter or more of projects studied by in-house analysts are classified as failures, damning evidence that billions of dollars are wasted, and if outside evaluations were used, the failure rate would be higher. By emphasizing the reality that many projects don't succeed, the staffers could curtail the relentless borrowing of poor countries.

Some defend the institution's dismal record by saying that at least the loans transfer resources from rich countries to poor ones. They also use this rationale to support the emphasis on maintaining loan volume instead of loan quality. Other Bankers defend the weak performance by saying that the global economy, the weather, or other unpredictable forces were at work. The projects were well thought out, they argue, but unforeseen circumstances took over. The argument is ridiculous on its face, overlooking the fact that many projects fail for a shortage of local management talent and a lack of recipient government will, deficiencies that should be foreseen by experienced professionals. Social programs are a good example of how problems are predictable, in that numerous social projects are forced on local governments, which, as noted, have few experienced educators, medical doctors, and community experts. Some of these countries prefer money for brick and mortar projects. With other recipients, the leadership consists of a small elite who believe the poor's principal potential is creating unrest; accordingly, social programs aimed at the reduction of poverty, illiteracy, and sickness—that is, programs that would strengthen the poor—are not high priorities. The Bank must cajole these governments into financing expensive social programs. They participate without enthusiasm, when their active cooperation is of crucial importance to success. When projects fail, the staff usually finds a culpable party among the consultants, contractors, other donors, or local governments. A regular target in this regard is the relevant ministry, which is described as "institutionally weak" or "unable to cope with the demands of competing agencies."

Like any group of people making their living in large bureaucracy, the Bank staff is urged on by considerations of job preservation, career advancement, and personal income. These matters become of paramount importance to the employees, who by reason of survival, check their integrity as development professionals at the front door. Personnel surveys indicate a high degree of job dissatisfaction among the staff, who complain privately of their frustration with the way things are. Status, prestige, and power provide solace to the group, yet given their high level of intelligence, academic curiosity, and desire to do good, one expects a greater vocalization of their concerns. The enduring silence of the staff is surprising.

These educated professionals submit to spending months inputting bland facts into project reports, which then must be endlessly rewritten to eliminate any speck of originality or hint of controversy. The slightest error is considered a major tragedy for its author, as the institutional culture supports the belief that one mistake jeopardizes a career. All too often, the reports fall into a cautious "tried and true" formula approach utilizing a stilted, legalistic jargon that is unique to the Bank and a few of its sister organizations, such as the Inter-American Development Bank. Regrettably, management's preoccupation with the written word places the loan report on a pedestal that is higher than the project itself. This preoccupation with words and format creates a high priesthood of individuals who know both the formal regulations and the informal nuances of the report making process. Over the years, a few individuals who are friendly with the Bank have expressed publicly the danger of clinging to this ingrained approach, which makes future changes more difficult. Moises Naim, a Venezuelan government official who served as an executive director for several years, noted this problem years ago when he told *Bank's World* magazine, that the Bank "is also an organization too heavily burdened by rituals and unwritten roles accumulated when the world was very different from what it is today."

Job Mobility and Compensation

It is not hard to see why the staff remains silent on the system's contradictions. Most are figuratively chained to their desks, depending completely on the Bank for their livelihood. They have little or no job mobility since the skills they learn on the job are unique to a handful of like institutions. Furthermore, for the three quarters of the staff who are not American citizens, their visas are restricted and require them to depart the United States within 30 days of leaving the Bank's employ. Should they desire to transfer to a responsible position overseas, their options are limited by the immigration restrictions prevalent in most industrialized nations, and the staff's native governments are less than friendly to returning Bankers. Home government civil servants, particularly in the Third World, have a built-in resentment toward their local brethren who put in substantial time at a Bank position, which is viewed as a high-paid "glamour" job far away from the day-to-day struggle in the trenches. Of course, the vast majority of employees have no desire to quit their jobs, even though they grumble about the institution. They are accustomed to the comfortable lifestyle afforded by the compensation packages and pleasant surroundings. And, as might be expected, after years in the United States, their families are thoroughly Americanized. A permanent job change involving a foreign land, particularly an undeveloped country, sounds unappealing.

The level of income and benefits provided to the Bank staff is attractive by any measure. New professionals, usually armed with a PhD in economics or another advanced degree, receive $80,000 to $85,000 in annual salary to start. This salary is free of any income tax, unless the new employee is an American citizen, in which case his pay is "grossed up" to reflect a calculation of his income tax and Social Security payments. The tax-effected salary is $110,000 to $117,000 annually. The perks are excellent. Five weeks vacation is standard for all Bank employees. Within six years, a professional can expect annual raises and two grade increases that bring his salary to the gross-up equivalent of $150,000. To this cash compensation must be added the substantial fringe benefits provided to non-U.S. nationals. Besides a generous health and retirement program (which all employees receive), the non-U.S-national staffer receives annual tuition grants of up to $12,000 for each child of school age and 75 percent of college costs for older children. The school subsidy enables the Bank's foreign nationals to send their children to expensive prep schools, while their American colleagues make do with public facilities. Regarding this benefit, a former director jokes, "You can't end the World Bank; half the private schools in Washington would close!" The college subsidy, which runs as high as $20,000 per year per student, is payable only if the child attends outside of the country in which the parent is working. It is not surprising that many applicants for overseas postings are employees whose children are near college age. For those staffers that stay in Washington, there remains the option of sending the children to a European or Canadian university. McGill University, one of Canada's best, is a popular choice. Foreign nationals also receive extra cash to fund family travel to their home countries. Taken together, the compensation package places many of the Bank's employees, who are essentially working for a charity, in the $200,000 range. This fact is shown in Exhibit 6.2 for an employee with one school age child and one college age child. If the employee uses his connections to get his spouse a development job, the combined amount increases accordingly, and places the couple among America's top earning households.

Exhibit 6.2   Compensation of Mid-Range Bank Professional

	Tax-free	Grossed-up Equivalent
Cash Salary	$110,000	$150,000
Education Grant	32,000	44,000
Home Travel Subsidy	5,000	7,000
	$147,000	$201,000

The staff is sensitive about the compensation and makes every attempt to compare the Bank's salary scale to profit-making companies. They avoid mentioning the private sector's attendant lack of job security and its attention to performance, versus the Bank's lifetime tenure and lack of accountability. Employees make 30 percent to 40 percent more in salary (on an after-tax basis) than U.S. Treasury workers with similar qualifications and they enjoy a superior vacation and benefits package. A typical Banker explains away the differences by pointing out that Bank salaries should be equal to those of other international bodies, such as the United Nations. This argument's underpinning conveniently ignores New York City's higher cost of living. Others make the questionable assertion that the differential is needed to attract quality personnel, despite the fact that the job application files are bulging and that turnover is a minuscule four percent. The low turnover shows how attractive compensation really is, relative to other available employment.

The combination of a high income and a secure job are just part of the incentive of Bank employment. Carrying diplomatic passports and holding the purse strings, staffers receive royal treatment from borrowers. And, as though money and status are not enough, those lucky staffers who become department managers receive the most obsequious in-house behavior from subordinates, who recognize that internal politics, rather than concrete results, spell career differences. This creates an interesting duality at the institution. Among the recipient country's finance ministers, a task manager walks imperially, for he is outside his superior's view. Standing before his boss, the same manager cowers. Occasionally, this authoritarian system reaches absurd lengths, such as the time when one of my colleagues picked up his director's maid in Mexico and personally escorted her to Washington.

The Club Mentality

Its unique privileges and cultural attributes turn the World Bank into a "club" for its employees, and not surprisingly, they can display an arrogance and moral righteousness that exhausts the patience of all but the most patient of observers. At a Washington cocktail party, employees can be found solemnly referring to the "The Bank," even to out-of-towners who have no idea of what bank they're talking about. As with any exclusive club, there is a long list of applicants and turnover is low.

Furthermore, certain people face discrimination in the club. For example, women make up 52 percent of the employees, yet less than one quarter of managers. Black professionals, meaning representatives of the African member nations, hold less than three percent of the jobs, and I have yet to meet a Black American in a professional capacity. Certain ethnicities band together to help each other out, showing the same tribal mentality that is discouraged in the borrowers. The Indian/Pakistani clique at the Bank is particularly effective in promoting its own. Informal internal estimates place those of Indian/Pakistani extraction (i.e., Indians, Pakistanis, Africans of Indian descent and so on), at 20 percent of the staff. Employees of other ethnicities make sarcastic remarks about the institution's "Indian Mafia."

The club adopts a fortress mentality over attempts to reduce the prerogatives and financial interests of its members. The guardian is the Staff Association, which is an elected employee delegation. Despite employee dissatisfaction with Bank processes, the Staff Association holds a remarkably narrow view of its responsibilities. During my six years at the institution, the Association fought two major battles with the Bank administration. The first dispute was a repeat performance on protecting the staff's right to use first class air travel. Every few years, management attempted to whittle away first class travel privileges, and the Association fought the changes. The Association's heated defense consisted of the argument that business class travel endangered the employee health, many of whom endure flights that last ten hours or more. While this "health" rationale was ludicrous, the Association's opposition was sound from the staff's point of view, since a downgrade to business class meant likely future downgrades to economy. The Association distributed "flying" memos to all employees on a regular basis. Eventually, management won and forced the selected use of business class.

The second donnybrook concerned the Bank's home leave program for non-U.S. nationals. The program originated with good intentions. Most employees are natives of countries far away from headquarters. Past managers wanted them to keep a cultural attachment to their homelands without straining the family pocketbook for long distance airfare. For years, non-U.S. nationals abused the home leave benefit, using the free airline tickets for vacations instead of home country visits. After controls were instituted to prevent the staff from avoiding their native lands on home leave trips, some exchanged the first class tickets for lower-priced excursion fares, and pocketed the difference in cost. Other employees figured out triangular fares that involved a brief stay in the home country, followed by a longer trip to a resort area. Management finally instituted detective measures to insure that tickets were used for their intended purpose. This move created a howl of protest from the foreign nationals, who considered their free airline tickets to be a right, rather than a privilege. After much discussion, the Association and management reached a compromise with foreign nationals receiving cash payments, in lieu of tickets.

The club's preoccupation with bureaucracy, benefits, and career advancement makes employees lose sight of poverty alleviation, and the staff's real concerns come through to the clients after repeated encounters. One Panamanian government official who worked with staffers on numerous occasions expressed her frustration this way: "Their goal is to develop countries yet they seem more concerned with their status in the Bank bureaucracy, their five weeks of vacation, the hotels where they're staying while on mission, and the restaurants where they're eating." And many employees privately agree with her. Over lunch, one colleague, who had a dozen years of increasingly responsible experience, confided, "After working here 12 years I don't believe the Bank is about development. It is about taking money from rich countries and giving it to poor countries, which then use the money to repay the rich countries." Some critics maintain that the Bank's insularity from its clients is one cause of the staff's disconnection. Seventy per cent of the employees live and work in Washington, far away from the problems of the Third World. One Bank engineer offered this variation on the "ivory tower" theory: "The economists start to believe they are God. After a few years in the Bank, they go down to these impoverished countries and immediately meet with the minister of planning or the minister of energy. He treats them well, takes them to lunch, and provides them with a chauffeured limousine for the week."

The disconnect extends into the monied background of staffers, many of whom, in my experience, lack empathy for poor people. About 60 percent of the professional employees are from developed countries and 40 percent from Third World nations. With its bias toward hiring people from prestigious (and expensive) universities, the Bank selects from a well-off applicant pool. One aspect of this pre-selection is that the institution's Third World professionals come from backgrounds far more elite than those of their U.S. and European counterparts. Only the richest of the rich from countries such as Ecuador, Egypt and Vietnam have the training to attend Harvard or Yale. A former colleague of mine from Nicaragua epitomized this notion, when he described his penchant for collecting $500 bottles of wine. This gilded upbringing, with its panoply of privileges, inures many to the day-to-day struggles of the poor, and poverty becomes an abstract notion rather than a practical problem grinding down real-life people. Such divides are promoted by the ability of non-U.S. nationals to bring servants on special visas that effectively allow below minimum wage.

Senior management's paranoia over loan volume and its dismissal of failed projects breeds a cynicism in even the most dedicated employee. Idealists who point out logical inconsistencies in projects past the birthing stage encounter disapproving glances. Continued objections lead to ostracism from meetings. Those who persist in not emulating the faceless, drone-like style of their superiors get a personnel briefing. Behind closed doors, they receive a lecture, as I did, on the importance of conformity in achieving a successful career.

Senior management is intensely conservative regarding new hiring. With one or two exceptions, the top 20 managers have each spent almost their entire working careers at the Bank. Indeed, as my first division chief pointed out, the institution has an informal policy prohibiting the hiring of experienced "outsiders" at levels above intermediate grade. This policy is harmful in two ways. First, it imposes severe limits in the exchange of fresh ideas that are vital to any organization. And two, it represents a self-imposed straight jacket on bringing in mature business people, who could be of substantial use in implementing and evaluating projects. Since it takes 10 years for an intermediate professional to reach manager status, any outsider after that period is an "insider," representing no threat to the ingrained culture. The ever-shifting executive director corps never stays long enough to pay attention to this problem, and the presidents traditionally delegate the implementation of personnel changes to career employees, a practice akin to having the inmates run the asylum.

VII.
THE BANK AND THE PRIVATE SECTOR

The World Bank has never been comfortable with the private sector. A large percentage of the professional staff has no business experience and have built their careers entirely at the institution. Most senior loan officers—who represent the front line of project approvals—received their doctorates at a time when central planning, rather than market-based theory, was popular at universities. They cut their teeth on projects for managed economies and gained little exposure to commercial industry, which they still consider anti-intellectual, sinister, and unappealing.

The initial impetus for integrating the private sector into Bank operations originated with the Reagan administration. In the early 1980's, national governments owned and operated large swaths of industry, and it was not unusual for significant components of telecommunications, energy, and manufacturing to be run under the central planning model. Services suffered relative to the free market alternative, and citizens lacked basic amenities such as adequate phones and electricity. At the same time, countries protected local businesses through direct subsidies and high tariffs, leaving the poor to overpay for necessities. Because few Third World countries escaped poverty, the administration attacked these arrangements as curbing growth, and criticized the Bank for propping up socialist regimes by loaning them money for parastatals, farm co-ops, and other central planning-inspired ideas.

The Bank resisted the Reagan Administration's private sector emphasis for three reasons. One, the United States proposed the idea, and the staff reflexively dislikes American input. Two, like any large bureaucracy, the World Bank resists change. And three, the administration took a narrow view of poverty's contributing factors, and some Bank executives believed the existing programs attacked the foundations of underdevelopment.

After eight years of U.S. persistence, a fading of central planning's acceptance, and the shifting desires of recipient countries themselves, the Bank implemented its "Private Sector Initiative" in 1989. From then on, authors of country economic analyses, strategy reviews, and project papers addressed the borrower's private sector and how the Bank encouraged it. For example, if Pakistan wanted an irrigation project, the related report posed a few stock questions:

- Was there a commercial financing alternative to the Bank loan?
- Did the loan support privately-owned water suppliers?
- Did the loan's conditions encourage the government to reduce its participation in irrigation?

In the beginning of the privatization makeover, the bureaucratic response to such questions was a brief section spouting nonsensical jargon like economic rents, institutional weaknesses, and non-tariff barriers. Following these bland comments were market-oriented loan conditions such as studying the sale of government monopolies, which as the reader now knows, had little substance even when the borrower did not completely ignore them. After a number of countries became more serious about private sector reform than the Bank itself, the staff jumped on the bandwagon by plying nations with adjustment loans designed, in theory, to finance the costs of transitioning a state-owned company into a commercial business. An embarrassing example of this "Johnny come lately" conversion was the Bank's inflated description of its role in Argentina's privatizations. In its *Development in Practice* publications, the Latin American Department indicated it "was a close advisor to government officials" and "supported the process with four new (since 1990) privatization loans." The attempt to claim credit for the Argentine experience was understandable because the privatizations were wildly successful. From 1989, when the Menem administration took over, to 1993, the country sold its principal public enterprises. Sales proceeds exceeded $22 billion and the government removed the firms' losses from its books. Prior to Argentina's privatization decision, the Bank was a major financial supporter of money-losing parastatals. From 1980-1989, for example, the Latin American Department approved nine loans totaling $1.8 billion to some of these same public companies.

During the 1990's, a privatization wave swept the developing world, and the cash proceeds to the selling governments totaled several hundred billion dollars. From the perspective of economic advancement, the outcome was mixed. The privatizations relieved the government of corporate subsidies and placed the public enterprises in commercial hands, where presumably the businesses became more efficient. At the same time, the privatizing governments, particularly in the former Soviet Union, encountered substantial problems. Lacking experience and under pressure to get things done, the countries sold when their economic situation was uncertain and their negotiating position was weak. This resulted in less than opportune sale prices, a situation that was magnified by the official corruption endemic to such nations, as valuable enterprises were steered to political insiders for pennies on the dollar. When completed improperly, the privatizations' transfer of wealth either enriched an existing elite group or created another rich class. In Russia, a particularly bad example, a naïve, corrupt and botched program placed a sizeable portion of the nation's industry into the hands of a few, newly-minted billionaires called "oligarchs." In 1992, 1994 and 1997, the Bank loaned Russia over $400 million for privatization efforts. Instead of providing cash, it should have demanded a slowdown to improve transactions, stop giveaways, and prevent wealth inequalities.

The metamorphosis from government financier to private-sector cheerleader presented the staff with formidable obstacles. From a technical point of view, the analysis required of a market-oriented project was far different than the analysis needed for conventional loans, and the economic benefits were often dependent on the vagaries of market behavior, which is notoriously difficult to predict even in advanced economies. Correctly evaluating and implementing such projects was a considerable challenge, and compounding the problem was the fact that the staff had few internal guides. Only a handful of senior personnel had meaningful private sector experience, and most staffers related poorly to corporate executives who could provide practical insight.

The minimal importance the Bank attached to giving advice on privatization was evident by the lack of commercial talent. Privatization group manager Kevin Young had been a World Banker since receiving his PhD in 1971. The Latin American privatization head had worked at the Bank for the previous ten years. The Asia Department's senior private sector development specialist had never worked on a privatization transaction. The director of the co-financing and financial advisory department, Ram Kumar Chopra, was responsible for the Bank's entry into commercial projects, but he had no private sector background and no expertise in evaluating large commercial financings. The vice president for finance and private sector development, Jean-Francois Rischard, ran the department that was most responsible for the private sector push. After receiving his graduate degree, Mr. Rischard spent 16 of the next 19 years at the Bank. The lack of business experience continues to this day.

The Bank and the International Finance Corporation

The principal commercial expertise of the Bank Group rests in the IFC, which makes investments directly in Third World private enterprises, without the benefit of a government guarantee. Despite operating for 50 years, the IFC has never been fully accepted by Bank professionals. With $13 billion in investment assets, the IFC is dwarfed by the $230 billion Bank, and the IFC's narrow private-sector objectives go against the Bank's more expansive multilateral-to-government role, which covers numerous economic, social, and political contexts. For decades the Bank considered the IFC as an insignificant appendage, and Bank managers privately derided the IFC staff as an intellectually inferior group that unwittingly functioned as a stooge of greedy Third World monopolists and exploitative multinationals. Similarly, IFC staffers have a low regard for their Bank brethren. Many IFC professionals have MBA's and some business experience; they have an executive's impatience with the Bank's academic theories and pie-in-the-sky lending programs. And, while both institutions have nearly identical owners and directors, they maintain separate managements, personnel departments, and employee career paths.

The differences extend into style as well. One personnel executive illustrated this point by imagining two identical offices in a Third World capital—one with a World Banker and one with an IFC executive. A visitor to the IFC office finds an outgoing individual with an outstretched hand and a willingness to serve a potential client. The same visit to the adjoining office encounters aloofness and annoyance. Instead of being greeted with a handshake, the visitor hears the World Banker announce, "I saw the minister of finance yesterday! Who are you?"

These disparate cultures ignored each other for many years. However, when the Reagan administration beat the privatization drum, it looked to the IFC, which had demonstrable commercial experience, as the vehicle to spur this policy. Fighting for its turf, the Bank fought off the attempt to enlarge IFC's input. During the Private Sector Initiative's design phase, the Bank was confronted with its shortage of business expertise, yet it limited the IFC to a consultative role in all Bank operations except financial sector development. Four years later, in 1993, the Bank opened a Financial Sector Development Department, with an 80 person staff and a processing capability that overwhelmed the abilities of the smaller IFC in this area.

In subsequent years, the Bank cooperated more with the IFC and certain similar departments, such as telecom, combined office suites. The Bank placed more of its resources in privatization and the IFC expanded its investment program. The IFC's status enjoyed a major boost in 2004, when another private sector initiative passed the Board and enlarged its role, but it remains on the sidelines during major policy discussions, country strategy reviews, and the like.

Role of the International Finance Corporation

The IFC provides long-term loans and equity finance to privately-owned companies. It refuses to accept government guarantees or to invest in government-controlled corporations, and it takes the same commercial risks as a bank lender and a stock market investor. If a borrower goes bankrupt, the IFC records a loss. If an equity investment declines in price, it loses money. The IFC's multilateral status reduces its political risks relative to a private investor. For example, the IFC has never had an investment expropriated by a member government and its borrowers receive preferential access to foreign exchange when a member government experience a hard currency shortage. Like its big brother, the World Bank, IFC funds operations by selling bonds in the international capital markets, but the IFC has never enjoyed the sovereign guarantees of the U.S. and the other G-7 shareholders. Despite its borrowing expense and emerging market orientation, the IFC consistently generates a profit. Over the last five years, the Corporation increased its investments at a 12 percent annual rate, but net cash outflows to emerging market companies—defined as disbursed investments less loan repayments and the book value of equities sold—remain small, reaching only $1.2 billion in 2006. Including IFC loans acquired by commercial banks raises this total to $3 billion, but it is a tiny figure compared to the $160 billion in 2006 foreign direct investment in the emerging markets.

In theory, the IFC has two principal roles: demonstration and catalytic. In its first role, it seeks to invest in developing countries that (a) are unfamiliar to large Western firms, (b) have poor track records with foreign investors and want to improve, or (c) have unsettled environments due to regime change. For example, the IFC was one of the first institutional investors in the former Yugoslav republics after their disastrous civil war. By going where others fear to tread, the IFC shows international firms that money can be made in emerging markets through the use of a conventional Western approach, rather than through government bribes, accounting tricks, and other shenanigans.

In its catalytic role, the IFC invites Western lenders and equity investors to share in the benefits of its multilateral status, which reduces the currency blockage and political risks of developing world investment. IFC extends long-term U.S.$-denominated loans at preferential rates to emerging market firms, and international banks buy portions of the loans, even as IFC remains the "lender of record" in the developing nation. Along the same lines, the IFC's equity participations provide comfort to investors that the recipient company "plays by the rules" and provides outside investors with a "fair shake." In effect, the IFC's catalytic role is a security blanket to those lenders and equity investors that like the emerging markets, but want to cut the risk of doing business.

Given these two roles, the IFC's assistance should only apply to situations where it is the "lender of last resort," i.e., where the company in question cannot find alternative financing at reasonable commercial terms. However, the evidence shows that the bulk of the IFC's financing goes to strong companies in a handful of select nations. These firms access money from multiple sources and consider IFC as one of several options. The Corporation's integrity in performing its demonstration and catalyst roles is thus seriously compromised.

Seven nations represent almost half of the portfolio, which leaves over 130 countries spread over the remainder. Six of the seven—Brazil, China, India, Mexico, Russia, and Turkey—hardly need the IFC's participation. See Exhibit 7.1. They are magnets for tens of billions of direct investment from Western companies and mutual funds. At best, the IFC can fulfill a niche role in these large economies, where it might support groundbreaking ventures or introduce Western innovations. Yet, the Corporation focuses on padding its portfolio with large loans to established firms controlled by wealthy elites and powerful multinationals.

Exhibit 7.1   The International Finance Corporation, Top Seven Countries by Investment Exposure

Country	(US$ Billions)	Percent of Global Portfolio
Russia	$ 2.0	9%
Brazil	1.5	7
China	1.5	7
India	1.3	6
Turkey	1.2	6
Mexico	1.1	5
Argentina	0.8	4
	$ 9.4	44%

Source: IFC Annual Report

For example in 2005, the IFC loaned $100 million to Tata Iron & Steel, a manufacturer owned by the Tata Group, India's largest conglomerate with over 96 companies. The Group is owned by the Tata family, one of the wealthiest in India (and the world) and not deserving of IFC's multi-million dollar subsidies. The loan was the fifth time the firm had hit the IFC well, indicating that the demonstration effect had finished long ago. In 2006, Ipiranga Petroquimica was another recipient of largesse, receiving $50 million in subsidized monies, the fourth time it had accessed IFC. Based in Brazil, the company is a joint venture controlled by Ipiranga Group—owned by five of Brazil's most prosperous families—and Hoescht A.G., the giant German chemical concern. This joint venture easily raises cash without the IFC's intervention. In Albania, the small country covered in Chapter 5, IFC's principal investment is with the local subsidiary of Britain's Vodafone, the world's largest cell phone operator by revenue, and not a charity case. These three deals are not isolated instances, but rather fit the norm. This activity neither alleviates poverty nor promotes growth; it simply makes the wealthy wealthier.

Because a large portion of the IFC's loan and investments can be completed commercially, the IFC is not a lender of last resort, and it actively competes with the private sector. Management's in-house justification for this strategy—besides preserving their own jobs—is that the blue-chip loans maintain the Corporation's AAA bond rating and permit more speculative investments in "frontier" areas, such as Cambodia, Tajikistan, and Tanzania. However, the fact remains that many international banks and finance companies operate with bond ratings lower than AAA, and so little of the IFC's portfolio is dedicated to frontier areas that the second argument doesn't wash. Furthermore, management's habit of placing poorly performing employees in the frontier investment departments, where loan volume is low and where they can't do much damage, does not bode well for a reversal of IFC's lending approach.

Contributing to the IFC's dependence on large, visible concerns is the institution's pressure to lend. At the beginning of each year, loan departments receive targets based principally on dollar volume, rather than innovative transactions in tough markets. Since an "easy" $100 million loan to a huge conglomerate in Turkey gets 10 times as much credit as a "difficult" $10 million loan to a fledging concern in Cambodia, department managers emphasize big transactions that meet the bulk of the budget. The portfolio then receives a sprinkling of complicated, small-country deals for cosmetic purposes.

Further reducing the catalytic role is management's view that the IFC must react to proposals brought before it, rather than to promote interesting investment ideas. The Corporation initiates few of its own transactions and relies on companies already familiar with the IFC to bring it deals. The resultant opportunity cost is depressing. With its experience in the developing world, the IFC has an ability to inventory a country's commercial environment and to marry small, local concerns with foreign know how, technology, and capital. Instead, a new business trip to Columbia, for example, consists of a loan officer seeing the nation's top 15 conglomerates and banks, most of which have access to commercial finance and most of which operate as price-gouging oligopolies. The IFC frowns on loan officers visiting U.S. and Western European companies in the hope of stimulating activity, despite the sharp rise in direct investment by such firms. Top management worries that the IFC's Third World shareholders view trips to business capitals like Chicago and Tokyo to be non-developmental and neo-colonial. This attitude is counterproductive and management has never offered a satisfactory explanation for it.

IFC professionals share the same pay grade, benefits package and job security as World Bank staffers, but they have separate career tracks and different backgrounds. As noted, IFC loan officers tend to have MBA's, rather than PhD's, and a far greater exposure to the business world, where closing deals and making money triumphs over economic theorizing. Nevertheless, the IFC, like the Bank, remains an insular bureaucracy, and memo writing, reading, and filing paralyze the transaction process. Virtually all high-level officers are lifers, with minimal experience in commercial banking or investment funds, and the Personnel Department generally prohibits the hiring of outsiders beyond intermediate-level jobs. The fastest promotion path is adapting to the "club" and making sizable loans to safe companies.

Although the typical IFC professional thinks that the IFC is "run like a business," that notion is delusional. No business could endure IFC's lack of productivity. In 2006, the institution had 2,400 employees that produced 284 new investments worth $6.7 billion. A reasonable assumption is that 75 percent, or 1,800 of the employees, work in the direct investment function as the IFC, unlike the World Bank, has no academic research facilities. The 2006 transaction ratio was one deal for every six employees, far worse than the two to three ratios I have observed in private industry. The poor productivity contributes to the IFC's high expense ratio. Relative to the direct investment departments of life insurance companies, which run similar operations on a domestic basis, the IFC spends three times as much on operations as a percentage of assets. This ratio increases to four times when account is taken of the fact that the IFC pays its non-U.S. employees on a tax-free basis, thus saving one-third on compensation costs.

The IFC's emerging market environment and missionary work, relative to life companies, inflates expenses so the true multiplier might be lower. But, when the IFC is matched on an "apples to apples" basis, the inefficiency is still apparent. Emerging Markets Partnership, a $5 billion private equity firm that specializes in the emerging markets, had about 150 employees during its peak investment phase. Applying EMP's assets-to-employees ratio to IFC's $13 billion in direct investments suggests 400 IFC employees rather than the 1,800 presently working in that function.

EMP's principal executives are ex-World Bank and IFC officials, which shows they can cut costs when they are owners seeking effectiveness, rather than bureaucrats seeking consensus.

For the last three years, the IFC's average net income was $1.4 billion and its return on capital was 15 percent. Because the Corporation pays no income taxes, this percentage is overstated relative to similar privately-run operations. Applying a normal income tax rate reduces the capital return to nine percent, which could not be tolerated in a commercial environment. Of the $4.2 billion earned since 2002, less than three percent went to free technical services for poor countries, a pitiful amount given the IFC's ostensible mission.

VIII.
A GOVERNANCE SYSTEM IN CRISIS

The World Bank's governance system is an ambitious attempt to marry a multilateral democracy with a large financial institution. It doesn't work. Staff supervision is inadequate, abuses remain unchecked, and non-accountability continues unabated. The founders' ideal of a rational development bank suffers as a result.

The governance system was established in 1946 and has changed little over the last 60 years. Designed to administer a modest reconstruction effort, it is inadequate for today's institution. Each member country is represented by a Governor (usually that country's treasury secretary, finance minister, or central bank president) and an executive director. A complicated formula allocates shares, and a country's voting power on corporate matters is weighted in proportion to its shareholding. At the IBRD, the United States holds the largest percentage of votes (16.4%), followed by Japan (7.9%), Germany (4.5%), France (4.3%) and the United Kingdom (4.3%). These five countries are the largest IDA shareholders as well. General oversight of Bank operations are the responsibility of executive directors since the governors meet only once a year. The president serves as chairman of the board and chief executive officer but he is subject to the general control of the executive directors.

The executive director position is a full-time job, resident at the Bank's headquarters and outside of its personnel regulations. Executive directors are on full salary and carry a staff of three to four professionals, including an alternate executive director. The full-time nature of the job and the related staff distinguish it most from the boards of directors of publicly-owned companies. There, the "outside" director slot is a prestigious but part-time position that does not merit staff support.

A Bank information brief outlines the arrangement:

Today the Bank has 24 Executive Directors. The five largest shareholders—the United States, Japan, Germany, France, and the United Kingdom—each appoint one Executive Director. The other countries are grouped in 19 constituencies, each represented by an Executive Director who is elected by a country every two years or a group of countries. The number of countries each of these 19 Directors represents varies widely. For example, the Executive Director speaks for six South American countries and another Director represents 22 mainly English-speaking African countries. The members themselves decide how they will be grouped. The country groups are more or less formed along geographic lines with some political and cultural factors playing a part in how they are constituted.

Based on the initial high rates of success, the system worked at first. The Bank processed just 10 or 15 projects annually in its early years and most were of the brick and mortar variety. The directors had time to study the proposed projects, interact with staff, and consider their votes accordingly. The United States was a far more powerful voice at that time and controlled the institution, which facilitated a measured governance style. As the operation expanded in size, scope and nations, the hands-on ability of the executive directors to oversee the operation diminished and the permanent staff played a larger role. The increased membership inevitably diluted the U.S. authority, which had provided the impetus for organizational objectives, and the new members' widely differing cultures and interests lessened the Bank's unity of purpose.

The public relations department trumpets the deliberative role of the executive directors yet the Bank has been a management-dominated institution for many years, the result of the executive directors being snowed under with paperwork. Under the existing set up, these 24 individuals are asked to consider almost every IBRD loan, no matter what its relative importance. They are further asked to consider almost every single investment project developed by the multilaterals founded subsequent to the IBRD—i.e., the International Development Association, the International Finance Corporation, and the Multilateral Investment Guarantee Agency. Piled on top of these transactional requests, which by themselves add up to hundreds of reports annually, are deliberations on the budgets of each organization and the myriad policy issues affecting them. Lengthy Board meetings consume two days per week, leaving only three days for other activity. The problem of the Board having time to evaluate seriously the many lending proposals, operating budgets, and policy issues is then compounded by the ponderous and jargon-filled prose in the Bank's memoranda, which, as the reader knows, also have a tendency to present risky projects through rose colored glasses. Finally, directors are constantly diverted by the ceremonial aspects of their posts, which have diplomatic status, and they spend considerable amounts of time entertaining visiting delegations, schmoozing with finance officials, and answering questions from the home office. One U.S. executive director griped that 30 percent of his time was spent on responding to U.S. treasury and state department requests for meetings and data. It is, therefore, of little surprise that the executive directors and their assistants are outgunned by the thousands of staff who prepare the Board documents.

The disconnect between the executive directors' oversight and the actual work being performed is heightened by the directors' short term of duty. Their appointments last just two years and the evidence indicates that this is not sufficient time for them to comprehend the Bank's arcane process and bureaucratic tunnel vision. Moreover, within the institution it is commonly acknowledged that no more than one-half of the directors devote sufficient time and effort to understand the nuances of its activities. This less-than-dedicated part of the Board is said to view the two-year posting as a resume-building diplomatic plum, where a job well done is difficult to accomplish and hard to recognize. This opportunism makes life harder for the Board's devoted other half and places substantial power in management's hands.

The voluminous paperwork, limited resource base, and short tour of duty conspire to weaken even the strongest director's resolve to make a lasting impact. At most, just one of 10 project reports is studied in more than a superficial way, and the budget and policy memoranda compete for the available time. As a result, most directors take a narrow view of their responsibilities. For example, in the case of the director representing South American countries, he might review only those loans related to his region. The director representing Japan might peruse only those projects in which Japanese companies have a chance at landing engineering contracts.

The directors' parochialism is supported, if not encouraged, by the constituencies they represent. The poor countries constantly vie for more of the cheap Bank loans. At the same time, the wealthy countries, which are not eligible for concessionary finance, fight to ensure that they receive an adequate share of the construction, consulting, and other procurement contracts created by Bank projects. The institution collects reams of statistics each year to determine which countries are the winners in the respective "loan" and "contract" derbies. This annual calculation is a poor reflection on the institution. Within and across the developed country and developing country blocs, the executive directors also work to see that allies receive a portion of Bank largesse. Thus, the United Kingdom executive director may work with the executive director responsible for Kenya, a former British colony, in lobbying for a new Kenyan loan. Likewise, the executive director representing Belarus, for example, might try to steer an engineering contract to Russia, a Belarus ally.

Directors are most powerful when they insert themselves into projects that are in the early going, before the institution and the borrower have committed themselves. When the projects approach the point of budgetary inclusion, the staff, the borrower and their respective Board allies adopt a "circle the wagons" defense against interference from other nations; and, thus, the influence of an executive director on a given project is usually effective at the margin. Over the years, this reflex has evolved into a "you don't criticize my project and I won't criticize yours" mentality, particularly among the Directors representing the poorer nations.

The principal exception to this rule has been the United States executive director, who is sometimes joined in this higher calling by one or two counterparts. Since the beginning of the Reagan administration, the U.S. director's position has been used, in an on-again, off-again way, to influence change. The principal U.S. thrust has been to promote the private sector. While this objective is already outlined in the Bank's charter, its implementation has been twisted and subjugated by the institution's desire to increase loan volume and by the staff's natural inclination to finance public sector ideals. The consistency of the U.S. privatization theme over a 25-year period, 1981-2006, has resulted in important changes in the manner in which projects are structured and evaluated, yet the staff's adherence to the underlying philosophy—i.e., that private investment and management is generally more productive than the public variety—has been impossible to achieve. In part, the U.S. "hit and run" approach has been self defeating, because it has not demonstrated the country's determination to further this principle on every project. Too many loans are pushed to advance a short-term American policy agenda. More importantly, the effectiveness of the U.S. director in promoting wholesale change is compromised by his own participation in the day-to-day horse trading and contract counting. When the staff sees the U.S. playing the same game as the other nations, it has one more excuse to portray an American reform cry as a superficial ploy to please Capitol Hill's anti-foreign-aid lobby.

No matter how much the U.S. suggests change, the governance system continues to encourage directors to back irresponsible loans. Consider the following: as a rich nation director, it is easy for you to score "brownie points" with the poor members by voting yes on bad projects. After all, most of the loans that you approve do not appear on your government's budget, and there is a real possibility that a corporation in your country (or constituent countries) will receive a lucrative contract as a result. Meanwhile, unless one is the borrower, your constituent economies do not suffer if the loan proceeds are ill spent. On the liability side, the Bank's own borrowing operations are conducted on a worldwide basis in multiple markets. The billions of dollars of savings that the Bank extracts each year to run its lending business are impossible to trace back to your constituents. Finally, the guarantee that your government has, in effect, provided to the Bank's bondholders is an off-budget item, and it has little chance of being called-in. The seamless web is complete.

The poor nations are tempted to "rubber stamp" loans just like their rich-nation colleagues for several reasons. One, objections that they raise regarding a loan requested by a competing constituent group invite retaliation. That is, they can expect problems on the next proposal for a recipient member of their group. Two, international bondholders deem the developing nations' guarantees of Bank debt as worthless. This fact lessens the poor nations' sense of responsibility for the Bank's obligations and gives their respective directors a freer hand in approving loans. And three, as a poor nation director, you might view the Bank's loans as a charitable donation, made by the industrialized nations to the developing countries. Everyone knows donations do not have to be repaid, and one

African diplomat characterized the Bank as a "Shylock" for wanting its money back. One exasperated Asian director confided to me this last sentiment, "The World Bank shouldn't make a profit and shouldn't decide on what loans to make. It isn't a bank. It's foreign aid."

With only one or two nations aspiring to rise above parochialism, the directors' inadequacy is readily apparent. The end result is a depressing state of affairs. The Board ignores the larger interest of economic development and fills its hours with trivial concerns that are far removed from the fundamental mission. This irrelevance is manifested in such pathetic activities as the directors impressing constituents by pestering staffers with impolitic questions and by holding up projects for reasons of gamesmanship. The Board's governance weakness is also manifested by its avoidance of key policy questions and its consequent inability to make decisions on the critical issues confronting the Bank—like the institution's expansive sense of mission, its limited resources, its high project failure rate, and its stratospheric expense structure—issues that top management is either incapable or unwilling to tackle. The directors' refusal to unite and perform a leadership role is a source of complaint within the professional ranks, who watch as important matters are routinely farmed-out to commissions and consultants for further study.

With the Bank's many problems, it is alarming that the directors do not take more action. Their refusal to adopt a meaningful oversight role and to go beyond the narrow interest of their respective constituent base is a breach of their fiduciary duty. By way of comparison, the responsibility of a public corporation director is more than representing one small group; it encompasses supervising the corporation's affairs in a manner consistent with a number of constituents, including stockholders, bondholders, customers, and employees. In the Bank's case, this constituent list must include borrowers, since they represent the majority of the shareholders. Few of the directors seem to recognize a fiduciary duty and it seems that most don't know what one is. This departure from accepted governance practice is best exemplified when directors fail to recuse themselves on deliberations regarding loans to countries they represent. About 30 percent of loan approvals, incidentally, are contrary to the Bank's charter, which stipulates that loans be provided with "due regard for credit."

In response to such criticism, the directors would likely respond as follows: "All the borrowers really need the money;" and, thus, they as directors can overlook conflicts of interest and credit problems. This "poor mouth" argument begs the question, of course, about whether piling more debt on near-bankrupt countries is a practical solution to poverty. Nowhere is there real proof that the directors initiated actions aimed at resolving this issue.

To some Bank observers, the Board's inertia is not surprising. The governance system, they say, is simply bureaucrats supervising bureaucrats. A background review of 21 directors and alternates was revealing. Thirteen of the 21 had advanced degrees in economics. Regarding professional experience, all 21 built their careers in the service of their respective governments, usually in the ministry of finance or ministry of economic development. Eight had employment histories in multilateral institutions such as the Bank and the United Nations. Seven had taught full time at universities. Incredibly, of the 21 resumes, only three indicated as much as one year of work experience in a private business. In fact, the group totaled 380 years of government, academic, and multilateral experience versus a miniscule ten years of business experience. In other words, the directors are pretty much like the Bank's higher-level staff—career civil servants far removed from the workaday world of real life.

The Board of Governors is not a substitute for the Board of Executive Directors. The governors are a more prestigious lot, in that they are ministers of finance or central bank presidents, but their managerial role is limited to ceremonial duties such as admitting new members, suspending old members, or increasing the capital stock. The governors meet just once a year, in joint session with the IMF's Board of Governors. This assemblage of economic power, known as the "Annual Meetings," takes place in a foreign capital and lasts a week to ten days. Traditionally, little is accomplished at these conferences. The 2006 Annual Meetings took place in Singapore, where the most notable action was the local government's reversal of its protester ban. Earlier, it refused to allow demonstrations, a basic violation of democratic principles. Due to the sheer size of the development community, the Singapore authorities closed downtown streets to local traffic to reduce congestion for the more than 10,000 diplomats, development professionals, and press officers in attendance. The governors and the assorted hangers-on at these meetings are characterized as lovers of the "high life" by Bank staffers. During the conferences, the majority that remains at headquarters likes to joke,

"Every limousine within a hundred miles of the Meetings is rented—and every prostitute within 200 miles!"

When the Bank was created, there was no evidence to indicate that the founders preferred a management-dominated institution. The fragmented ownership and democratic objectives instilled by the charter, however, encourage a weak Board. Further undermining the directors is management's uncanny skill at deflecting outside pressures through using public relations, co-oping critics' agendas, and shifting focal points. Bank employees carry diplomatic status, and they refuse to testify before the legislature of any shareholder, including the U.S. Congress. In fact, the bureaucracy seems answerable to no one.

Perhaps the only solution to the governance problem is a strong chief executive who could act as a counterweight to the deep-rooted staff. Unfortunately, the prospects of a president running the institution with an iron fist are remote. The last president who truly controlled the organization was Robert McNamara. He arrived in 1969, when it was a far smaller and simpler institution. For example, when McNamara took over, the Bank had 1,600 employees and $12 billion in loans. Today, the Bank is a massive enterprise; it has 8,500 employees and $230 billion in loans. McNamara hired huge numbers of people who were personally loyal to him. Today's president takes office with minimal flexibility on new hires and immediately confronts an ossified bureaucracy with an ingrained culture. McNamara's drive, initiative, and sheer energy molded the institution, but his changes were not accomplished over a short period of time. He served 13 years, the longest term of any Bank president.

According to an unwritten agreement, the United States selects those individuals who serve as the Bank's top executive for the standard five-year term. Employees believe the U.S. considers the top job to be a retirement post for political patrons of the ruling party, and the lunchroom wisdom is that the appointees come to the Bank looking forward to a cushy job with a lot of embassy party invitations. Once they arrive, they learn there is a lot of hard work. Not ready for the onslaught of meetings and paperwork, the president withdraws from the fray and important matters are handed over to the permanent staff people. This cynical inside view is in obvious contrast to the news copy generated by the public relations department, which creates dozens of "photo ops" for the president as he travels abroad. The unfortunate truth is that the cafeteria gossip is mostly right. The last four top executives have had little impact on the institution's fundamental direction and have shown even less interest in the essential problem—the Bank's unending drive to continue making more loans for more projects that don't work.

In defense of the presidents, it should be noted that they start off with one hand tied behind their backs. In fact, the "Bank president" title is a misnomer since the occupant of the office has few of the powers of a commercial bank president. For example, immediately upon assuming the job, the President learns that he faces a passel of fiefdoms—with leaders that don't talk to each other. By silent agreement, the groups do not object to each other's loan proposals, but they do compete for volume and to get their proposals in front of borrowers quickly. This conflict crosses geographical lines as well as sector groups. The new president finds it impossible to fire managers who disagree with his philosophy because of the rigid personnel policies. Likewise, staff members cannot be transferred under duress, even at the President's express instruction, without lengthy administrative hearings. He finds it difficult to bring in more than a few outsiders; hiring regulations discourage new blood at positions higher than entry level. With the exception of a few directors closely allied to American interests, he finds little support for change from directors; they owe him no personal loyalty and back the status quo. Finally, he confronts a bureaucracy so well situated that his directives are disarmed and subverted with impunity.

Even modest reform proposals put forth by the new president encounter tough sledding. Before formal consideration, they run through a tortuous decision process taking months and years. Bureaucratic delay is the polite word for the sabotage that is the institution's reaction to meaningful reform. The president finds himself a lonely dilettante, standing opposite a cadre of Bank officers unified in the belief that they know the development business and they manage the organization, not the president. The staff's resistance is understandable. They are tied to the Bank and are unlikely to find similar high-paying employment. If reforms mean slower advancement or outsider hirings at upper levels, the staff suffers. Situated alongside the staff's naked self interest is its disdain for both the president's political allegiance to the United States and his work experience outside of the aid community. For those employees who have canonized themselves in the pursuit of poverty alleviation, the president is a stain on the institution's white robes and his office carries no legitimacy.

Clearly, the job of World Bank president is more akin to that of a university president who supervises a large group of tenured faculty, or to that of a politically-appointed head of a government agency who wrestles with career bureaucrats. Senior Bank staffers, indeed, see themselves as the true custodians of the institution's policies, and Bank presidents, who come and go, as temporary nuisances. With little opportunity to bring in their own people or adopt their own management style, the presidents are stuck with the reorganization as the primary means of change. By changing job classifications and unit designations, favored staffers get moved to influential positions. The various Bank reorganizations over the last 25 years complicated organization charts and played havoc with career paths, but the basic business was not affected. Veteran personnel simply removed from one position in the bureaucracy to another, an expensive version of musical desks.

In a mega-crisis like the Southeast Asian currency collapse of 1997, the U.S. Treasury exercises sufficient influence to make things happen quickly. But the end result of that effort was more loans, which the Bank favors anyway.

In short, the institution has outgrown its governance system. The principle of global cooperation, so important to the founders, has been achieved but the Bank's primary mission, promoting the economic development of its member nations, has not. Given this background, it is surprising that the operations continue without the fratricide that is endemic to the United Nations, another sizeable multilateral. True, the Bank functions smoothly, with only an occasional protest from its primary members, but the negative effects will keep compounding until no amount of good intentions can paint them over.

IX.
THE END OF THE WORLD BANK?

L ike the dinosaurs of old, the World Bank is huge, slow-moving, and unable to adapt to changing circumstances. It is making its way to irrelevance, to be followed by the threat of extinction. If left neglected, there is no reason to keep it alive. As one multilateral executive put it, "You could close the Bank tomorrow, and the effect on the global economic system would be zero."

Shutdown is Not an Option

Of course, in Washington, DC, bureaucracies are almost never shut down, and the Bank's gift for offering something to just about everyone delays the day of reckoning. Wealthy nations provide foreign aid without tax growth, poor countries get soft loans without policy change, and staffers receive premium compensation without accountability. Lobbying for the institution is a large assortment of "Beltway Bandits"—businesses, consultants, and nonprofits that also prosper from the development gravy train. Arrayed against the special interests are a handful of underfunded do-gooders and ideologues trying to make a difference. The balance of power is clearly in the Bank's favor, yet the specter of poverty, and its two stepchildren—terrorism and failed states—gnaw at the institution's foundations and its members' resolve in preserving the status quo.

Proposed Reforms

In the present day, the optimal approach—gutting the institution and starting over—is unrealistic. But people of goodwill should favor improvements that do more than nibble around the edges. A list of such proposals include the following:

A True Lender of Last Resort

For those countries that can access debt markets on their own at reasonable terms, the Bank should refrain from further lending. As others have pointed out, these countries do not need the Bank's money and their involvement boosts loan volume at the expense of real development. The change would allow the institution to return to its origins as a lender of last resort, which means it will not compete with private capital.

The near-term implications of the new policy will be fourfold: (1) a sharp drop in loan volume; (2) a commensurate staff reduction; (3) a drop in profits; and (4) a lowering of the bond rating. A reasonable expectation of the volume decline is one half in the next few years, but that's not all bad, since cutting off the creditworthy recipients frees up cash for the harder cases. On the basis of less activity, substantial layoffs will be required, even after compensating for the fact that troubled country projects require more investigation. As the portfolio shrinks, the Bank's interest income will diminish faster than expenses, hurting profitability. At the same time, its exposure to the poorest countries will rise, and a few former recipients might use the loan stoppages as an excuse to renege on their obligations. The cumulative effect of these factors will heighten the perceived riskiness of the Bank's bonds, and a reduction in the rating from AAA to AA seems likely, even with the guarantee of the wealthy members. Most of the ratings impact will be felt in the Bank's investment trading business, where it stands to make less money with a higher cost of funds.

Narrow the Project Focus

Reducing the number of borrowers will sharpen operations, but shareholders should demand that management reduce the assistance agenda as well. At present, the institution allocates aid to over a dozen different sectors (see Exhibit 9.1), with each having a half dozen sub sectors. Loans fall into more than 70 project categories, causing problems for the staff in compiling sufficient experience and expertise to serve clients effectively.

Exhibit 9.1 Existing Project Sectors

Agriculture
Education
Energy and Mining
Finance
Health and Social Services
Industry and Trade
Information and Communications
Policy Adjustment
Poverty Reduction
Public Administration
Transportation
Urban Development
Water and Sanitation

At most, the Bank should focus on four sectors, and thus, it could make fewer, and perhaps larger, loans to the smaller recipient base. Indeed, one multilateral executive thought four sectors was excessive, "all the development banks should select different themes and put all their eggs into one or two baskets; it's the only way any of them can be effective." Given the Bank's high marks in physical infrastructure, it seems obvious that agriculture and transportation are good choices. Education and public administration (i.e., corruption) are likely options as well, although their vague outcome measurements are problematic.

A bonus to this tight agenda is the promise of more time for the finance ministers of the low-income countries. Right now, with multiple loans to multiple sectors from multiple development banks, the time they allocate to aid projects is monopolized by process, rather than results.

Scientific Measurement and Outside Audit

Outside observers, both sympathetic and antagonistic, have urged the Bank to institute a verifiable scientific system for measuring benefits. Management has resisted these suggestions for years, with the tacit connivance of many members, but such a system is urgently needed. The immediate effect of scientific measurement will be a large decline in social projects.

Similarly, the Bank's policy of grading its own operations, to the exclusion of anyone else, has to stop. Staff must define a limited number of statistical outcomes for each project, and subject those outcomes to independent scrutiny. The firm hired to perform these assessments should then be rotated every three years, to lessen its dependence on Bank fees and to forego any temptation towards partiality.

Bring in Business Experience

With the world looking for market-based solutions to public policy problems, the Bank is woefully undermanned in terms of business experience. This does not have to be the case. Given the gravity of the poverty issue and the attractive compensation of the institution, it is not unreasonable to presume that private sector executives, perhaps in mid-career, might wish to devote a few years to the Bank and its challenges.

Overhaul the Governance System

The time has come to strip the Bank of its governance system, which distracts from the mission through inertia, ineptness and parochialism. After the focus is narrowed and the statistical measures are installed, the shareholders can dispense with full-time directors and, as former Bank vice president Joseph Ritzen has said, "Get rid of the diplomatic control of day to day management." Assuming effective guides are devised, the Board can meet for a few days at the end of each quarter.

At the same time, the number of directors should be reduced from 24 to a more manageable number, such as 15. To promote diversity and fresh thinking, member governments should consider appointing a few prominent businesspeople, rather than following the usual practice of nominating political insiders and finance ministry officials. In fact, a few Board seats might be reserved for independent directors, free of government shackles and bureaucratic ladder climbing aspirations.

Encapsulated Projects

Aid projects need to be supervised and controlled more closely than is currently done. My experience in business and in development indicates that the risks and rewards of Bank loans approach those of early-stage companies. Accordingly, it seems reasonable that the staff institute incentive, supervision, and monitoring tools that parallel some of those used in venture capital. The idea is to give projects some of the attributes of an entrepreneurial business—speed, efficiency, and focus.

Under the present set-up, the Bank diffuses its negotiating position with recipients by making smallish loans to multiple sectors. Those projects that do have a corporate flavor lack the requisite controls. Concentrated resources could dominate a single sector and strengthen the Bank's hand in promoting adherence to its procedures and measurements.

Spin-off the Research Department

The research arm of the Bank covers a number of different departments, which together employ 1,000 people who prepare studies and academic papers. Like any scholarly setting, the work has an uneven quality. Some papers are very good. Others push the Bank's ideological agenda, relying on selective statistics and dismissing counter arguments. Because of the primacy of volume, researchers have minimal influence in the Bank's operations, which are dominated by the loan departments whose projects can contradict existing studies. This disconnect advocates a stand-alone research function, free of Bank bureaucratic ties, and relieved of its obligation to toe the party line.

As others have proposed, members could use a portion of the Bank's retained earnings to endow new poverty think tanks. For one billion dollars, the institution could originate two foundations with 200 professionals each, and assemble two boards of directors with blue chip pedigrees and multiple disciplines. A location in Washington, New York, or London could be complemented by a Third World site, such as Sao Paulo, Lagos, or Jakarta.

Shrink the International Finance Corporation

The IFC competes with Western investors in big countries like Brazil, China, and India, when it should emphasize transactions in the smaller nations where multinationals and global funds are reluctant to commit. When it does invest money in these riskier countries, it should cease its annoying tendency of allying itself with large concerns that can take care of themselves. The Board has blinked at these practices for too long, and it is time for the IFC to re-enter the development business. First and foremost, the IFC should end new investments in the healthiest nations, with the only exceptions being novel demonstration projects, such as its support of collateralized mortgages in Mexico. Secondly, the IFC should curtail the practice of supporting multinational ventures and local oligopolies in the smaller countries. Most of these businesses access finance on a reasonable commercial basis, and the IFC loans to them are thinly disguised subsidies to the already wealthy.

At the start, this action will affect the IFC in the same way as the Bank returning to lender-of-last-resort status: lower investment volume, lower profitability, a lower bond rating, and fewer staff. Management will cut the IFC's ballooning expenses and consolidate its far flung offices. With headcount substantially reduced, the remaining employees will confront a challenging environment, and good deals will be hard to find. Correspondingly, they will work with companies that truly need assistance and with projects that have a valid developmental purpose.

Along with operational changes, the directors would do well to consider two policy directives that have broad application.

Currency Substitution

The typical developing country currency has a poor record of holding its value, contributing to cycles of inflation, panics and recessions that bedevil the Third World. This situation is disruptive of a nation building a modern economy. To weaken this phenomenon, the Bank, for most of its smaller recipients and a few of its larger ones, should insist that the local money be replaced with a hard currency, such as the dollar, Euro or yen. The implications of this transition have been the fodder for a number of academic papers, but at base level, the change would instill confidence in financial markets that lean toward speculation and uncertainty.

A hard currency regime will be a tough sell to those Third World politicians who complain of neo colonialism. They have legitimate concerns, but the Euro has shown that nations act as sovereign entities even when sharing the same currency. There is no reason to believe that such worries cannot be worked out for poor nations.

Agriculture Reform

Bill Gates, Microsoft founder and head of the $30 billion Gates Foundation, notes, "Today, no country of any size has been able to sustain a transition out of poverty without substantially raising productivity in the agricultural sector." One way of supporting that goal is to provide the vast armies of farm workers with a sense of ownership. Right now, a tiny elite controls much of the arable land in the emerging markets. Acquiring a portion of their holdings at fair value, distributing it to the poor, and equipping the new owners with the requisite training and materials is achievable in smaller countries, assuming concerted effort among foreign aid donors. Japan, South Korea and Chile are three countries with successful track records in land redistribution, but the topic is a touchy subject in development circles. It causes resentment in the Third World's upper class, which has a disproportionate influence, and injects anxiety into Bank professionals, who fear that backing any distributive scheme, no matter how sensible, forever labels them as "socialists." That is a career killer.

A second approach is for the rich nations to boost Third World crop activity by opening their markets to additional imports. Farm lobbies routinely kill this idea, but if they sacrificed just 10 percent of their protection, the resultant trade activity would provide employment for millions of poor people.

The reforms suggested for the Bank apply to its regional cousins as well—the Inter-American Development Bank, the Asian Development Bank, the European Bank for Reconstruction and Development, and the African Development Bank. Any push for a Bank makeover has the spillover benefit of sparking discussions about the remaining institutions.

Reforms Benefit Wealthy Nations

Increasing the effectiveness of development banks will be very advantageous for the wealthy nations, which run up huge costs fighting poverty's stepchildren—terrorism and failed states. Since 2001, for example, the U.S. has spent $80 billion on one problem country, Afghanistan, the Taliban stronghold. Most of these dollars go to defense rather than development.

The political capital expended in fixing these institutions will be large, but the related cash costs will be small. Both will be worthwhile investments for the major stockholders. Follow-on successes in poverty alleviation will pay big dividends in the form of avoided defense, homeland security, and immigration costs. If a revitalized Bank prevents one Afghanistan, the return on investment might easily exceed a thousand to one. The old saying, "An ounce of prevention is worth a pound of cure," sums up the opportunity.

Who Leads the Charge?

Despite the financial attractions of improving the Bank, the Western governments are unlikely to take the lead in serious reform. The U.S. has the most to gain, but its track record indicates a profound reluctance to push needed change, and getting the top five shareholders—the U.S., Japan, Germany, France, and England—to agree on anything is difficult. The borrowers have a different outlook in bettering the Bank, but they are also fractured. History shows that even modest proposals must run through the formidable gauntlet of the Bank's public relations, lobbying and foot-dragging machine, which has defeated any number of constructive suggestions. The hesitation of shareholders is thus understandable.

It is from outside the government and the development industry that change must come. A wealthy industrialist with an interest in fighting poverty is the logical choice to get the ball rolling. Only this kind of individual can marshal the resources necessary to highlight the problems, publicize the solutions and engage the opinion leaders. Based on my experience in public advocacy against well-entrenched interests, the industrialist will have to spend one-tenth of the Bank's public relations budget, or $8 million annually, to force serious improvement. A sensible time horizon for a desired outcome is five years, or $40 million. As the new generation of billionaires steps into aggressive philanthropy, this particular battle may attract one or two of them.

Closing

A few months into writing this book, I interviewed a former consultant, now living abroad. His words are poignant: "The organization has a lot of shortcomings, but the world would be worse off without the Bank, or something like it." I agree with this assessment. In proper hands, the multilateral model can work, and there is time for the Bank to use productively the attributes conferred on it by sovereign nations. At present, the institution is a wasting asset, sowing the seeds of its own demise. Whether it can reverse course is an open question. To paraphrase poet Robert Burns, "the best-laid plans of mice and men often go awry," and the World Bank may be another testament to this axiom.

INDEX

The letter *e* following a page number refers to an exhibit on that page.